'The title exactly reveals what this book is about. Many books have been written about how to develop a family business, how to sustain it, and how to be successful. This book is different. It is the first book ever to thoroughly apply the solution-focused approach to the field of a family and its business. Cauffman pours his more than 25 years of experience into a format that is didactic, informative, and highly readable. The storyline of the John and Annie family runs from the inception of the business to the arrival of the third generation. In between, the reader is effortlessly provided with many tools; useful insights from the solution-focused approach and updated best practices for the protagonist, his family, non-family family managers, and the company's strategy.'

Prof. Mr. Jozef Lievens, *lawyer and family business consultant, Managing Director of Belgian Family Business Institute, FFI Fellow*

'This is a special book that is written not for a professional audience or a business family, but rather one that is designed for both. Advisors can use it to add the solution-focused approach to their expertise, develop their own toolkit and work with families, while families can use it to look ahead to anticipate and prepare for each developmental challenge that is destined to emerge. This is a special book that will help so many advisors and families to chart their future, and deal with the deep and special family bonds that lie at the core of their shared life project.'

Dennis T. Jaffe, Ph.D., *research associate at Wise Counsel Research*

Developing and Sustaining a Successful Family Business

This practical and important book offers ideas, examples, and suggestions that address the challenges inherent to developing and sustaining a successful family business. It explores the complex dynamics involved in working with loved ones and how to pass a business on to a new generation.

Structured around the story of a family that has built a successful enterprise, now facing the issues of succession, the book utilizes the solution-focused model to provide step-by-step instructions to creating good working relationships and orienting toward common goals while building trust, respect, and love.

Complete with summaries, toolkits, and case studies, this book is an essential read for any member of a family business, as well as those who provide services to family businesses, including coaches, consultants, and non-family employees.

Louis Cauffman is a business economist and clinical psychologist with a wide range of therapeutic training, ranging from Systemic Family Therapy to Ericksonian Hypnotherapy through all possible directions within the solution-oriented approach.

The Professional Coaching Series

This series brings together leading exponents and researchers in the coaching field to provide a definitive set of core texts important to the development of the profession. It aims to meet two needs – a professional series that provides the core texts that are theoretically and experimentally grounded, and a practice series covering forms of coaching based on evidence. Together they provide a complementary framework to introduce, promote, and enhance the development of the coaching profession.

Titles in the series:

Swings and Roundabouts: A Self-Coaching Workbook for Parents and Those Considering Becoming Parents
By Agnes Bamford

Internal Coaching: The Inside Story
By Katharine St John-Brooks

Coaching in Education: Getting Better Results for Students, Educators, and Parents
By Christian van Nieuwerburgh

Coaching in the Family Owned Business: A Path to Growth
By David A. Lane

Integrated Experiential Coaching: Becoming an Executive Coach
By Lloyd Chapman

The Art of Inspired Living: Coach Yourself with Positive Psychology
By Sarah Corrie

For further information about this series please visit https://www.routledge.com/ The-Professional-Coaching-Series/book-series/KARNPROFC

Developing and Sustaining a Successful Family Business

A Solution-Focused Guide

Louis Cauffman

Routledge
Taylor & Francis Group

LONDON AND NEW YORK

Cover image: © Getty images

First published 2022

by Routledge
4 Park Square, Milton Park, Abingdon, Oxon OX14 4RN

and by Routledge
605 Third Avenue, New York, NY 10158

Routledge is an imprint of the Taylor & Francis Group, an informa business

© 2022 Louis Cauffman

The right of Louis Cauffman to be identified as author of this work has been asserted in accordance with sections 77 and 78 of the Copyright, Designs and Patents Act 1988.

British Library Cataloguing-in-Publication Data
A catalogue record for this book is available from the British Library

Library of Congress Cataloguing-in-Publication Data
Names: Cauffman, Louis, author.
Title: Developing and sustaining a successful family business : a solution-focused guide / Louis Cauffman.
Description: New York, NY : Routledge, 2022. | Series: The professional coaching series | Includes bibliographical references and index. |
Summary: "This practical and important book offers ideas, examples, and suggestions that address the challenges inherent to developing and sustaining a successful family business. It explores the complex dynamics involved in working with loved ones and how to pass a business on to a new generation"-- Provided by publisher.
Identifiers: LCCN 2021047312 | ISBN 9781032046785 (hardback) | ISBN 9781032045603 (paperback) | ISBN 9781003194200 (ebook)
Subjects: LCSH: Family-owned business enterprises. | Family-owned business enterprises--Registration and transfer.
Classification: LCC HD62.25 .C384 2022 | DDC 658/.045--dc23/eng/20211116
LC record available at https://lccn.loc.gov/2021047312

ISBN: 978-1-032-04678-5 (hbk)
ISBN: 978-1-032-04560-3 (pbk)
ISBN: 978-1-003-19420-0 (ebk)

DOI: 10.4324/9781003194200

Typeset in Times New Roman
by MPS Limited, Dehradun

Illustrations by Fjodor Schafranski

"To the real John and Annie. For all the John and Annies in the world."

Contents

Foreword xi
What Is This Book About? xv
Author's Introduction xvii
Dramatis Personae xix
How It All started xxi

1 A Family Business Framework 1

2 A Solution-Focused Framework 12

3 Family and Family@business Life Cycle 18

4 Education Is the Mother of Leadership 38

5 The Big Question 48

6 Challenges for the Next Generation 57

7 How to Prepare G1 for Succession 64

8 The Solution-Focused Toolkit 73

9 The Solution Tango 88

10 Conversations with the Siblings 102

11 Next Gen: Eight Tools for Your Future 118

12 Generational Transfer, Sale, or IPO? 129

13 The Decision of a Lifetime   141

14 The Dance of the Stakeholders   146

15 G1 How to Let Go after Succession?   156

16 Three Family@business Governance Tools   164

17 Three Family@business Management Tools   174

18 The John and Annie Family Business, Ten Years Later   190

*Addendum 1 Little Note on Solution-Focused Mediation
for the Family@business*   198
*Addendum 2 Is the Solution-Focused Approach an
Evidence-Based Model? YES!*   199
Bibliography   200
About the Author   203
Index   205

Foreword

Family business can mean many things. While those that are long-lived and gigantic make the news, the real story of family business are the millions of small household ventures – stores, restaurants, services – that are owned and operated by a small but growing family. At the next rung of the ladder are larger enterprises, started by family members, that have grown to be profitable pillars of the community. They offer a wonderful livelihood for the family and a place that contains the family's dreams for the future. But that dream does not come automatically or easily. After achieving success in its first generation, the entry, employment, and succession of each new generation are fraught with challenges and potential pitfalls. Is the next generation competent, motivated, and prepared for leadership or should the family quit while it's ahead?

This is not a business problem, as this wonderful volume makes clear – the rewards but also the responsibility lies with a family whose relationships, values, and culture embody the business.

The Solution-Focused Family Business Guidebook is just what it says – a resource for a business family to take with them as they go on this journey. It is not a business book; it is a book about the underside of the business. It is about the family business, but the author is a family therapist, a profession and a way of looking the struggle for a family to grow and change. A family is designed for stability – to resist change and maintain stability. But when the family owns and operates a business, the family needs to learn how to adapt, grow, and change to meet new conditions.

But this isn't a therapy book either. The unique challenges facing the business family stem from their family dynamics, but they are also business related. The family business straddles two worlds: family and business. Each is a human system that operates with different goals and intentions. The family is biological, and its purpose is to nurture and develop a new generation. It is focused on protecting parents and growing but undeveloped children. You are a family member eternally. Not so a business, which is based on results and conditional. You are a part of it when you meet expectations. While coworkers care about each other, in some cases to the point where they feel a bit like family to each other, they are not families, together for life. A family business must allow members to move from the nurturing caring family system to the more demanding and conditional business system. It is hard to have two roles – father and boss, daughter and employee, brother and sister, and business owners. This is the drama of the family business but also its unique advantage over other businesses. By caring about each other, knowing and trusting each other (when the family is working), family members can be adaptive, responsive, and effective with the demands of a business.

Family business advisors, and business families, are not seeking therapy; they seek help with business problems facing their families. The professionals who work in this field span several different professions – law, finance, accounting, business strategy, estate planning, and family counseling. Like many in this field, including the author of this book, I have a background in more than one area. Like the author, I was trained and licensed as a clinical psychologist who originally practiced family therapy. But, also like the author, I also have a business degree and spent many years working as a business consultant, helping large and small businesses deal with culture change. With these two areas of focus, I am able to understand the business needs and also to help families implement their strategies.

The work described in this book begins with a model taken from a family therapy, but it is forged, refined, and then applied to the unique and challenging needs facing a family business. This is not therapy, but a unique endeavor of dealing with business challenges that are overlaid and aggravated by family dynamics. The solution-focused model, as described here, is uniquely able to deal with these issues. This is the first book that introduces technology and tools for family, business, and individual growth and change that is derived from the expansion of this innovative approach to deal with family business challenges.

This guide takes the family as its center and outlines the progression as a family births a business and raises it to adulthood. It presents the emerging challenges clearly, and how family members can grow and adapt to continue to find success.

The book is large and complex, but it is grounded in a story – of John and Annie, and their growing business and three children, from their birth into the third generation. It is about relationships having to change and grow. The book presents each stage of the development of their family and business, and documents how they faced and resolved each challenge.

The book begins with their dream – starting a business, and also building a family. They are deeply connected but also separate, each with their own demands. John and Annie take on separate roles, always interacting and responding to each other. The rest of the book, taking place as their three children develop their own paths and take on various roles in relation to their now thriving and growing business, offers a complex and incredibly important story. It is not only about how they overcome each obstacle and maintain both their deep family connection and business effectiveness, but how they do this on a day-to-day basis. The book introduces several family advisors who teach the family what they need to know and guide them to actively face and resolve differences as they emerge.

In the detailed narrative, we see the family work through issues following a family-systems-based model of solution-focused learning. While this model originated with family therapy, this book extends the model outside the world of therapy into the even more complex world of family business. Through helping John and Annie and their family, the book also provides lessons for other families who are embarking on this journey.

This book can be read and absorbed in different ways. One can read and learn from the story of John and Annie or can look at how their story illustrates the evolution and life cycle of a family business. Or a reader can focus on the policies that a family can use to anticipate challenges and plan for the future, or as an advisor to learn how to work with a family in these areas. It is many books together, each one offering a different lens into helping families.

Along with the stories of the family and how they learned to communicate, make decisions, and change and adapt their roles vis-à-vis each other, the book offers tools for other families to resolve each issue. While what faced John and Annie was their own personal journey, their journey goes through each of the common steps that are commonly faced by a business family. They prepare their children as they become adults, offer a possible place and role in the business, deal with the difficulty of working as parents and children, and owners and employees, and eventually pass control to the next generation and step aside. The book presents each stage and after following the personal story of one family, allows a family to look at itself and use the tools they have learned.

This is a special book that is written not for a professional audience or a business family, but rather one that is designed for both. Advisors can use it to add the solution-focused approach to their expertise, develop their own toolkit, and work with families while families can use it to look ahead to anticipate and prepare for each developmental challenge that is destined to emerge. This is a special book that will help so many advisors and families to chart their future, and deal with the deep and special family bonds that lie at the core of their shared life project.

Dennis T. Jaffe, Ph.D., is a research associate at Wise Counsel Research, and author of several seminal books on family business, including more recently **Borrowed from your Grandchildren: The Evolution of 100-Year**

Family Enterprises, and **Cross Cultures** (coauthored with James Grubman). Over a long career, he has advised hundreds of business families and trained and mentored generations of family members and advisors.

What Is This Book About?

John and Annie

Throughout the book, you will be in the front seat to observe how the family and business lives of John and Annie, their children, and employees evolve from a young couple to a growing family and from startup to full-grown company. You will learn how the children gradually become involved in the company up to and including the moment when they take over the leadership from the parents.

It is obvious that after several generations, many more people are involved and the complexity of the business poses more challenges. This book provides a framework for handling these complexities.

Individuals differ from each other and the same is true for families and family businesses. No case is the same. Yet, comparable dynamics are often at play. The John and Annie case can be seen as a template that you can fill with the specific details of your own situation.

Future Proof Toolkit

Starting a business is one thing, making it successful over the generations is of an entirely different nature.

In order to avoid the infamous three-generation trap "from rags to riches to rags," meticulous precautions are necessary. The biggest challenge for a successful family@business surely is the transition over the generations. This book serves as a guideline to help both the Founding Generation and the Next Generation to take the necessary steps to maximize a successful outcome.

Foundations of This Book

The author was the first to translate the innovative solution-focused approach for use in management, coaching, and other business applications. This is the first book ever on the application of the Solution-Focused Model for family@businesses.

It contains the author's expertise after more than 30 years of study and service to family@businesses.

Theory and Tales

In the first part of the book, we put more emphasis on explaining the professional expertise that is useful when working with, for, or in a family business. This part of the book is more in the form of a textbook. In the second part of the book, the many dialogues show how it works in practice. This part is more in a conversational style but the reader can easily translate the storytelling into a more formal textbook.

Just like the intertwining of the life cycle of the family and the family@business, the tools of the solution-focused approach are interwoven with best practices, conversations, theoretical insights, practical applications, and the evolving story of the John and Annie family into a tapestry of many colors.

How to Read This Book

The order of the chapters follows the logic of the different steps in the life of a family business: from birth of the company, growth into a complex organization, and succession by the next generation. However, the reader can choose to go through the chapters he needs most at this point in his career.

Terminology

We introduce the concept of family@business to highlight the intimate connection between the family dynamics and the business dynamics that make family-owned companies special.

Throughout the book, we will call the Founding generation G1 and the second generation G2 or Next Gen.

Author's Introduction

When I studied clinical psychology, my dream was to become a therapist, preferably a very good one. I had the chance to work in a university hospital in a newly founded family therapy unit. None of us had much experience but we were allowed to follow as much trainings as we wished. Those were the days…. So, I traveled extensively for workshops and internships. We began inviting international experts to come and teach in our center. This gave me the chance to work with and learn from the big names in systemic family therapy at that time.

In the early 80s, our practice got – serendipitously – an influx of family therapy cases that were a bit out of the scope of our regular clientele. Used to working with chronic psychiatric patients and their families where we had reasonably good results, we considered these new clients as easy cases. They had work, no one was in the hospital, no psychiatric symptoms, financially well off, and with – in our well-meant but rather a disrespectful view at that time – problems that we considered more as inconveniences. But we were flabbergasted that we were not able to offer much help to them. As psychologists, we were totally focused on relationships and emotions within the family. Working in a systemic way, we obviously asked people what they did for a living. When someone told us they were self-employed, we took notice of the fact and did not further go into this. It took us time to realize that these families all came from a family business background. Being self-employed could mean that the person owned a shop, but it also could mean that the person was the owner of a company with 250 persons working for him. Once we discovered the importance of the company as part of their system, we started asking questions about the family business and the relation with the family. We discovered that many, if not most, of the family business families looked upon the family business as the eldest child of the family. That was an eye-opener. We discovered that talking about the business and how the family related to those issues opened gateways to their healing. We were criticized for this. Many colleagues in the academic world frowned upon the notion that family and business matters could be related.

One world was psychology, the other world was business and they were not to be mixed.

Intrigued, I decided to study economy and management to learn about the inner workings of a corporation. Although in the mid-80s there was little interest in family business, I choose this as my field. I discovered that family businesses were and are the pillars of the worldwide economy. My fascination turned me into a family business enthusiast. Many family businesses found their way to my office, both with relational challenges and with business dilemmas. Founded in 1986, the Family Firm Institute was and is the world's number one organization dedicated to the study of and support for family businesses worldwide. In 1990, I was invited to give a workshop at their New York conference. I was able to build a large practice, combining psychology with business. At the same time, I met Steve de Shazer and his wife, Insoo Kim Berg, the founders of the Solution-Focused Therapy model. I was one of the first to invite them to Europe (1987) and we collaborated closely until their passing in 2015–2106. Steve and Insoo who were strictly into psychotherapy were astonished how I translated their model as a business application. Hundreds of family business cases later, I founded an international training institute that serves both the clinical field and the business field. My focus remains on serving family businesses. The book that you hold in your hands is the accumulation of 30 years of studying, learning, experiencing, coaching, consulting, writing, and teaching in the field.

I hope you have as much fun reading as I had while writing this book. Enjoy!

Dramatis Personae

The Company: Solution Builders International
  The John and Annie Family
  Parents:
    John and Annie, Co-Founders and Co-Owners.
  Siblings:
    Eric, future CEO
    Ella, M.D., Urologist
    Cherly, future HR Officer
  In-Laws
    Lars, husband of Eric
    Max, husband of Ella
    Pablo, husband of Cherly
  Grandchildren
    Eric and Lars: Esther and John Jr.
    Ella: The twins, Aurora and Annette
    Cherly: Indra

  The Family@business Consultants
    Mark: Psychologist, Family Therapist, Business Economist, developer, and trainer in solution-focused coaching for the family@business
    Cynthia Hange: Professor Organizational Design and Innovation

  The Non-family Family
    Bert: employee number 1
    Alice: employee number 2

  The Management Team
    CFO: Muriel
    Head Marketing: Alice

HR and Legal: Lillian
Country managers: Bruce, Gunther, Alessia, Jacques, and Chen
General Manager: Jerry
Investment manager: Mony
Business Unit managers: Monika, Andrea, Patrick, and Rebecca

How It All started

Half-past two in the afternoon. The front door slams. John storms into the house, face red, mood ferocious. Annie, his wife who works from home as an accountant, is startled: "What's wrong? What happened?" John grunts something incomprehensible, pours himself a stiff drink, and gulps it down.

Pacing back and forth, fists clenched, John tells Annie: "*I have had it with these F&$%heads, I quit. My manager killed my project. Told me I have been tinkering long enough with it. He even used the word "played with it," the moron. I will never ever set a foot in that place again, never. Unless to buy it. Taking me off my project, who do they think they are.*"

Annie knows her husband well enough to let him ramble, curse, and use ugly words until his steam runs dry. She knows that her working day has ended and another work starts: getting John at ease so that they can talk sense.

Having met at the university where she studied finance and he was in engineering, they married right after graduating. The week after John got his Ph.D., their son Eric was born. Headhunted out of his postdoctoral program, John works as a project manager in a multinational. Besides his day job, John spends all of his free time developing a software program. It is his dream to write a software package that will fully integrate all the back-office functions that construction companies need. He has been raving about this project to Annie for some time now. How the software will interface and integrate all elements of the building process. How the libraries of all possible building materials and subcontractors will speed up the quotation process. How the project management module will interface with the performance studies per component and of the whole building process as it goes along. How inventory can be minimized by a continuous synchronization with the progress of the construction process. John realizes this is a distant dream but he keeps going at it with all his passion. Annie helps him with the financial and fiscal aspects of the program. They both know that their product, when ready, is scalable.

Annie: *"So, tell me why you go bonkers."*

John: *"We got summoned to a meeting and our manager simply told us that he pulled the plug on our project. It was way too slow and too expensive, he told us. But he hasn't got a clue and does not understand the importance of this project for the future of the company. It is not the first time that he acts like this. Well, I lost my marbles, got mad and yelled at him. When he told me to get out, I really lost it."*

Annie: *"Oops. I can imagine how that must have looked like."*

John: *"Yeah, I exploded and told him to stuff his project."*

Annie: *"Then what?"*

John: *"I left the building and I intend to never go back."*

Annie: *"So, we need to talk about our future then! Let's go for our own company."*

The result: after a few days of doubts, hope, and calculating, they decided to start their own business. Annie was confident in the feasibility of John's concepts. John was confident in Annie's financial managerial know-how. Their shared dream: becoming entrepreneurs.

They had some money in the bank. Annie would continue working as an accountant. That would pay for their daily needs while John would immerse himself in speeding up his construction software.

The apartment became a beehive for the growing family and the startup business.

Buckle up and let's go for a ride!

Chapter 1

A Family Business Framework

A Short History of Family Business

In the beginning there was difference. And then there was light. And then, after a long while there were *Homo Sapiens*. The early *Homo Sapiens* were hunter-gatherers, constantly on the move to find edible crops and prey. Gathering crops was mostly reserved for the female members of the clan whereas the – allegedly – stronger male clan members mostly did the hunting. This forced them to operate separately and in small units. Learning new skills and obtaining novel knowledge was kept to that small unit, a clan, so the progress of learning was difficult and slow. Cooperation with other clans was necessary to survive. After all, where –before the invention of deep freezers – did the clan that killed a mammoth kept the rest of the meat that they couldn't eat themselves? In the belly of the other clan, by sharing it in the hope that when the time comes the other clan would share too. So that when their time came to be hungry while the other clan had been lucky in the hunt, they got some leftover meat in exchange.

Sometime later, as population grew, *Homo Sapiens* developed an agricultural society that allowed much more food production, social stability, and the creation of a "homeland," which diminished the need for constant travel. There also was less need for separating men and women in their work, so clans slowly could evolve into genetically related units a.k.a. families. In parallel, *Homo Sapiens* developed first language and then writing. Brain development allowed *Homo Sapiens* to think and dream about things that were not there in reality, the so-called symbolic representations. For example, cave drawings show the products of this development. Now, most *Homo Sapiens* became farmers that soon found out to – cleverly – specialize in different crops so that quality and quantity became better. Then they started bartering within their local society. But after the invention of money, they could deliver their goods to far greater distances because payment by a symbolic representation of value (a.k.a. money) facilitated a diversity of trade. With the invention of debt, doing business became possible over vast territories and with a great diversity of other, even unknown *Homo Sapiens* in distant locations. So, the invention of language, writing, money, and the concept of debt made rapid outward expansion

DOI: 10.4324/9781003194200-1

possible, even unavoidable. The growth exploded with the leverage tool of debt, a promise fueled by money and trust.

With large group cooperation in networked systems that span vast territories, trade grew exponentially. Local products were exchanged via an ever more complex trade network that allowed local goods to be traded for more exotic goods. Over ever more complex levels of go-betweens, interactions between people who did not even know the other one existed, became possible. The world opened itself. An important inward movement mirrored this outward movement: the growing importance of the family. Father taught his son how to trade or how to grow whatever the father had specialized in or whatever the mother fabricated at home. The family, the family home, and the family working together became a haven of safety, trust, and prosperity toward the future. The Family Business was invented.

From One-Man-Band to Family@business

The vast majority of companies start off as the initiative of individuals. Only after this venture survives the first dangerous years of the company's existence – mortality rates in the first five years are high – can we speak of a viable company. Ownership and exploitation are in the hands of one or a few persons. If this company keeps going and growing, there will come a time when children or other relatives become involved in it. In the literature, there are more than 30 different definitions of a Family Business, but they all have the following in common: a Family Business is owned and run by members of a nuclear family.[1] The size of neither the company nor the fact that it is privately held or listed is irrelevant.

What is relevant is that a Family@business is a hybrid organizational form where a business system and a family system overlap. The challenge is to accept their differences and exploit the combination of two systems, one based on economic principles and the other based on emotional ties. Simply stated: Family ⟷ Business. Or sharper:

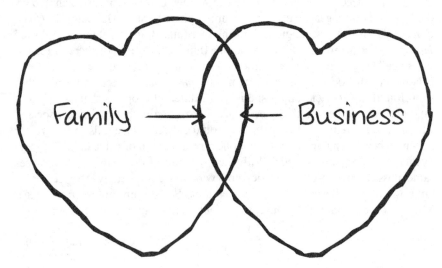

Family Businesses in the World

Family Businesses are the driving force behind the global economy. According to the Family Firm Institute, the world's leading association for family enterprise professionals, family-owned companies account for two-thirds of all businesses worldwide, generating more than 70% of global GDP annually.

Yet the general public and even the business community underestimate their economic importance. The size of the family@business is of lesser influence than the complexity of the family and the business. There are worldwide very big companies that the public often doesn't know that they are family-owned.[2] These companies are well known because they sell directly to the public and therefore use their name as a brand.

The absolute majority of family-owned companies are suppliers or service providers to other businesses. Their names are mostly unknown except to their customers. Yet they can be very big and important in the market. Professor Hermann Simon discovered companies that he calls "Hidden Champions." Their characteristics are: within the top three in the global market or number one in their local market determined by market share combined with low-level public awareness. In other words, those Hidden Champions are "the World's best unknown companies." Besides the world-famous brand-name companies and the hidden champions, there are millions of family-owned companies that do their work in silence and in the background. Yet they are the backbone of national economies worldwide.

If you take the time to look for family@companies, you will enter a wonderful world that goes much further than listed multinationals that often have anonymous owners.[3]

The Family Business Is the Eldest Child

The young company needs a lot, if not all the time, attention, and passion of the entrepreneur in order to make it viable. The company and its growth into a successful enterprise create the identity of the entrepreneur. Very often, the Family Business is like the eldest child in the family. It is the center around which everything revolves, and which provides the income, the security, the status, the future, and a meaningful occupation to every member of the family.

Everybody lives for it, through it and of it. Yet, this "eldest child" can't take care of itself. On the contrary, it needs the constant, full, and undivided attention of the entrepreneur. The family is organized around the business. This gives meaning to all involved and provides money, togetherness, meaning, respect, and prestige.

All these elements create the huge differences between Family Businesses and large non-family (listed) corporations. In the latter, top management,

HR, and the executives continuously must move heaven and earth to create involvement and loyalty of the workers toward the corporation. In a family business, loyalty and involvement are (almost) self-evident.

In order to work with and for a family business, this "company is the eldest child" issue is of the utmost importance. If outsiders, non-family workers, and professionals providing services to a family business fail to appreciate these emotional bonds, they will not be successful in their co-operation with the family business.

Atomic Power

The family aspect in a Family Business is like atomic power. Atomic power can be used to fuel a nuclear power plant, but it can also be used to create an atomic bomb.

Working with the ones you love is a powerful motivation to go further and faster. The family ties combined with the passion for the company makes coworkers capable of going the extra mile. Success in family@business and success in succession are defined by good relations. The crucial ingredients are trust, communication, harmony, and respect. Without this the family ties are distorted and working with your family can turn into an emotional and economical hell.

Generation to Generation

Starting a business is relatively easy, making it viable is not so easy, growing a business is a lot harder but successfully handing a business down to the next generation and surviving that transition is the most difficult step.

Everybody can start a company; making it big is not given to all, and only a few exceptional people can make a company flourish over several generations. Yet, family businesses are vulnerable. Worldwide statistics show that the mortality rate[4] among family@businesses is about 15% at the end of the first year of existence and some 23% after the second year. Having survived the dangerous initial years, roughly one of three family businesses make it into the second generation. Only one out of ten makes it from the second to the third generation. These numbers deteriorate further: 3% make it from the third to the fourth generation and only 1% from fourth to fifth generation and beyond. The average life expectancy of family businesses is 24 years, which more or less coincides with the period in which the founder of the company is actively present.

Succession planning therefore is critical for the survival of a family-owned business in the face of such stark numbers.

Family@business Challenges

Regardless of how small or big they are, all family-owned companies or family@business, as we will call them in this book, struggle with the same challenges that stem from the combination of a family and a business:

1 How to combine the rational world of a business and the emotional world of a family?
2 How to flourish as a business and as a family?
3 How to survive as a company while the leadership changes over the generations?
4 How to deal with the double-edged sword of ownership and management succession?
5 How to work with the ones you love?
6 How to involve non-family and other stakeholders?

Uniform answers to these fundamental questions are simplistic and therefore counterproductive. These fundamental questions do not have simple answers. On the contrary, the answers to these questions must be tailored to each individual, each family, each company, and each family@business. As you go through this book, you will find partial answers everywhere that you can put together to find the best answers to suit your personal situation.

Reading guidelines

Question 1 is dealt with in Chapter 2, where you will discover the intimate link between the family life cycle and the business cycle.

Question 2 is dealt with in segments of Chapters 3, 5 and 6 where we describe the importance of education, the challenges for the next generation and the preparation for the phase-out of G1.

In Chapter 10, where we explore the tools that the next Gen can use to prepare for their future success, we provide answers to question 3.

The building blocks for addressing question 4 are described in Chapter 12, where the next generation finds crucial information for their own future, and in Chapter 14, where G1 learns how to gradually pass on their life's work.

Question 5 is dealt with in Chapter 9, where the siblings are confronted with each other because their cooperation forms the basis for the future of the company and if they fail, this might be the end of the harmony in the family (and the end of the company).

Since a family@business -unless it is a very small organization- cannot be managed without 'outsiders', it is very important to find respectful and effective ways to invite the 'family outsiders' to become part of the family@ business. Chapter 13 provides best practices on how to work with stakeholders, while Chapter 16 provides practical tools that help family and non-family collaboration in such a way that it is beneficial for the business.

Family Business Succession

When the time has come to think about handing over the business to the next generation, a double challenge opens up. Throughout this book, you will find several toolkits for dealing with the complexities of both challenges.

The first challenge is to find the equilibrium between serving the future of the business and serving the interests of the family. In this process, it is important not to forget the other stakeholders: spouses, siblings, important non-family family executives, employees, customers, suppliers, the general community, etc. All stakeholders deserve the appropriate attention at the right time.

The second challenge is to simultaneously handle the inheritance succession and the management succession. All too often, when people think and talk about business succession, they limit themselves to the legal, fiscal, and financial components of the inheritance. All too often avoiding inheritance taxes together with making the take-over affordable for the successor is the only goal. When the company and the family have a certain level of complexity, this monomaniac stance can be a precursor for disaster. Obviously, the correct and legally optimized inheritance, meaning the transfer of money and shares, is important. As the legal, financial, and fiscal practices are different in every country, we will not deal with this technical component. The good news is that the expertise that you need for these technical components can easily be bought locally.

The other component, the transfer of power and the succession of the management of the company prove vital for the future of the company.

Succession Is a Process

This process is characterized by an interactive dynamic between founder-owner and successor: G1 leaving the scene in style and G2 resolutely entering the stage, G1 slowly fading into the background, and G2 determinedly taking up more responsibility. In short, the concern is with transferring and taking over. When you carefully consider the words "transferring and taking over," you get a good idea of what is essential: it requires proactive behavior from both parties. Metaphorically speaking, it is like digging a tunnel from different sides of the (generational) mountain and then meeting each other in the middle.

Though the best financial, fiscal, and legal experts surround G1 and G2, they still need to wade through this emotional, relational, and psychological minefield.

Succession Is the Bridge to the Future of Your Company

Crucial for the success in the succession process is that the interpersonal relationship between all parties involved is strong enough to withstand the unavoidable stressors of this transition phase.

Ten Best Practices for Creating Good Relations

The following recommendations will help you build and maintain the best possible working relationship for working with the ones you love. All best practices are interconnected and stem from the value that guides human interactions: respect. As you read the book, you will encounter many practical examples in the many dialogues that the John and Annie family will have as they move through time.

1   Give and earn trust
    Founders-Owners are – by nature – entrepreneurial doers with strong personalities. Since they created their company out of (almost) nothing and did this (almost) all on their own, most of them have difficulty in letting other people do things their way. This goes for employees, staff members, and certainly for the children who step into the business. When you have been the sole driver of the car for a lifetime, you have made it through many difficult navigational situations, then it is not easy to allow a younger person – with much less experience in (business) traffic – take the wheel. Let alone, to feel safe while sitting in the passenger seat. What you need here is trust that the other can and will do a good job, although in a different manner than yourself. However, let's be frank: although the love for your children is very deep, that shouldn't lead to blind trust. There simply is too much at stake. Trust needs to be built. The transferring owner offers his trust and the successor earns the trust to become the next captain of the family business. Nothing is more reassuring for a transferring parent than a successor who shows his/her entrepreneurial drive.

2   Accept mistakes
    Perfection is not of this world. It is unavoidable to make mistakes in both life and in business. Working with the ones you love is a long learning process, as you will discover in Chapter 2. As the family life cycle unfolds in parallel with the business cycle, you inevitably end up with dilemmas, difficult choices, decisions that you have to make on gut feeling for lack of experience and, inevitably, you will make mistakes. Entrepreneurship cannot take place without risk and therefore making mistakes is a normal part of the "Game of Business." Entrepreneurs accept this and learn from those mistakes under the motto: better make a mistake than do nothing. Both parties, G1 and G2, realize that the process of transferring and

overtaking demands a learning process and that making incidental mistakes is as unavoidable as making mistakes in the education of your children.

3 Respect differences

All people are different and think, do, and feel in many different ways. It is counterproductive to try and smooth out those differences. "In this family, we all must do X, like all the rest of the family. In our company, everyone acts like Y, like all the rest of the company." This all-flattening posture creates animosity and smothers diversity. Like in Nature, diversity is necessary if you want robust, adaptive, and healthy family@business development. So, accept and respect differences between the generations, within the generations, between the members of G2 and within your personnel. Your family and your family@business will profit.

4 Accept conflicts

A taboo on conflicts can result in the buildup of an emotional volcano that – sooner or later – will erupt. The more energy is pent up, the more devastating the consequences will be. Since people differ, have their own ambitions, want things for themselves, like to take credit for their own accomplishments, it is only normal that conflicts occur. There is no fire without friction. It is what you do with the fire, what you do with the conflicts, and how you handle them that is of importance. If conflicts end in a zero-sum game (one wins, the other loses) nothing constructive will come from that in a family@business. Zero-sum games are good for sports such as Ping-Pong, Tennis, or Chess. But the Game of Family@business is very different from those games. If, on the other hand, one handles a conflict such that it becomes a non-zero-sum game (you win, I win too), then the circumstances are there to turn conflicts into positive happenings. An example: two brothers disagreed over a business investment. The disagreement turned into a conflict. They went through a difficult time. When they noticed the negative effect of their conflict on their personnel, they chose to have a constructive conversation with the help of a mediator, an uncle they trusted and who had nothing to do with the company. The result was that they canceled the investment, reorganized the business, and went on the lookout for other opportunities.

5 Keep in contact

When you work with the ones you love, it is normal that, besides the joy of working on a common goal in your family@business, you will encounter frictions, annoyances, tensions, and disappointments. Being family and working together can at times become too much and now and then you will need some distance, both emotional and physical. If, however, this distance turns into a division, trouble lies ahead. If you no longer find the courage or the energy to invest in the contact with the ones you love and work with ("I am so busy, no time for small talk and by the way, what I do myself, I do better…"), you will drift apart rapidly. When this happens, you risk losing the capacity of an immediate (re)connection when things run badly. A proper contact tolerates distance while a proper distance creates space for creative cooperation.

6 Use constructive criticism

In most cases, parents love their children and vice versa. Parental love can blind you to the fact that your children, like yourself, are not perfect. Especially when children fulfill the deepest wish of Founders-Owners of a family@business, for example, to come and work in the company with the outlook of taking over in a later phase, this parental love can block, or at least, hamper objectivity. Parental love should not be blind but forgiving and yet clear when it comes to constructive criticism. Never criticize with the aim of putting people in a negative light. Always criticize with the aim of making people better.

7 Stay close to yourself

Children can be so full of admiration and even awe for what their parents have accomplished, that they show socially desirable behavior in order to please their parents, even if this goes contrary to their personal convictions and values. If you allow this admiration to blind you, your future and the company's future is likely to be compromised. The awe for parental authority should not lead to stiffening adoration or copycat behavior. There is no value addition for personal, family, or business purposes in freezing your own personality. Face your own values, act upon them, and enter a constructive conversation where differences surface within your family. Do not allow your personal or family sensitivities to get in the way of common sense.

8 Practice the art of giving compliments

In the macho world of business, some people strongly but wrongly believe that giving compliments is something for softies. This is a big mistake. You only have to take a moment for yourself and think about the last time somebody gave you a genuine and authentic compliment. How did that feel? Remember the last time you gave a genuine compliment to one of your coworkers. How did she respond? It made her feel good. It made her feel respected. A simple truth: when you feel good because other people make you feel good, you perform better in whatever you are doing. It is obvious that giving compliments has nothing to do with flattery, which is counterproductive.

Giving compliments always works on two conditions: you have to be authentic in what you offer and the compliments have to be relevant to the situation. Authenticity (almost) speaks for itself. Relevance means that the compliments you offer must be appropriate to the situation and based on reality. An example; when you conduct your yearly appraisal interview, it's hardly appropriate to compliment your employee on his well-shined shoes or on her nicely manicured fingernails (unless of course you are the manager of a shoe shop or a nail salon).

> Every compliment yields a dividend

9   Cherish your resilience

Life is an adventure, interspersed with joy and adversity. So, setbacks, misfortunes, hardships are part of life, be it as an individual, as a family, and as a family@business. Therefore, it is helpful to realize that we have a special resource to help us wade through difficult moments: resilience. Resilience is a quality of all human systems to deal with disruptive life events, overcome them, and learn from this experience so that one is better armored for when the next disruptive life event comes our way. Examples of disruptive life events: being born, dying, sickness, dismissal, leaving home, relocations, family arguments can turn into family feuds, divorce, bankruptcy of clients or suppliers, failing products, workplace accidents, etc. This list is endless. The endlessness of this list is a limitation for which there is no solution. The only thing we can and need to do is use our resilience to accept, overcome these disruptive life events, and learn from them so that we as an individual, as a family, and as a family@business become stronger.

10   Communicate

The most powerful tool for solving problems and challenges is constructive communication[5]: asking, listening, talking, discussing, and continuing to listen. Approaching the other with an open mind and being curious about what he has to offer is the ultimate basis for cooperation and opens up opportunities that you probably would never find on your own.

> Constructive Communication is the conveyor belt of ideas and feelings that feed good relations.

Notes

1 Commisioned by the European Union, the Expert Group on Family Business finetuned the following definition that is accepted worldwide. www.europeanfamily businesses.eu

A firm, of any size, is a family business, if:

1 The majority of decision-making rights is in the possession of the natural person (s) who established the firm, or in the possession of the natural person(s) who has/have acquired the share capital of the firm, or in the possession of their spouses, parents, child or children's direct heirs.

2 The majority of decision-making rights are indirect or direct.

3 At least one representative of the family or kin is formally involved in the governance of the firm.

4 Listed companies meet the definition of family enterprise if the person who established or acquired the firm (share capital) or their families or descendants possess 25% of the decision-making rights mandated by their share capital.

2 To name a few: BMW, Peugeot, Volkswagen, Fiat, Ford, Porsche, Ikea, Aldi, Carrefour, Novartis, Huawei, Samsung, LG, etc.

3 The following Internet portals give you wonderful access to the world of family@ business.

If you like to see where in the world which family@business is operational, click: http://familybusinessindex.com/#map

Do you prefer the latest update (2019) of the top 750 biggest family@businesses? Click https://www.famcap.com/the-worlds-750-biggest-family-businesses/

Interested in the top 500 of privately owned companies in China? Click https://finance.sina.com.cn/zt_d/2019_mq500qbd/

For in-depth background information you can visit www.FFI.org, the website of the Family Firm Institute that is the leading association worldwide for family enterprise professionals and the organization of choice for the advisers, consultants, educators, and researchers who help perpetuate transgenerational family business enterprise.

4 Due to the complexity of the family@business world, there is not a single definitive study that reveals the one and only true number. Numbers on the percentage of family@businesses differ per country, per continent, per decade, small- and medium-sized versus large family@businesses, privately owned versus listed companies, etc. The methodology that is used to crank the numbers is different for every study. It speaks for itself that the numbers on mortality rates throughout the generations are even more difficult to track. By the way, from a solution-focused perspective, we prefer the term survival rates☺.

5 Unfortunately, there is also destructive communication. With destructive use, communication can lead to tensions, conflicts, adversity, misfortune, hatred, and even war. Destructive communication can undermine the harmony in the family and make a successful family business nearly impossible.

Chapter 2

A Solution-Focused Framework

In the beginning of the eighties, Steve de Shazer and Insoo Kim Berg developed the solution-focused model in the context of psychotherapy. Since then, the model has spread rapidly and it still continues to do so. The solution model not only spreads rapidly within the original field but also in many other fields of application. This is possible because the solution-focused way of thinking and working is a process model. In itself, the model is without content. The content comes from the client and the situation at hand. This accounts for the remarkable applicability to all kinds of work contexts. As a result, the solution-focused model found an application in many professional fields: psychology, education, coaching, management, etc. Now, the world of family@business embraces it.

We are happy to share the endorsement that Steve and Insoo wrote in 2001 when my book on solution-focused coaching was the first publication to discuss the use of the solution-focused model in business.

In grateful memory of Steve and Insoo

DOI: 10.4324/9781003194200-2

Over the years, we have been pleasantly surprised, or rather shocked, that the approach has found appeal in fields other than therapy. It had never occurred to us that the solution-focused way of doing things could be applied to management, education, supervision, and team building as well as other areas of human endeavor. Louis Cauffman, it must be pointed out, was one of the pioneers in developing a solution-focused approach to these other fields. We are really impressed that he has been able to keep it simple and not give in to the all too human urge to make things more complicated than they need to be. Like any good solution-focused therapist, Louis Cauffman keeps his techniques unobtrusive within the context of a strict business environment and thus they are often unnoticed. Rather, the ideas and techniques of solution-focused brief therapy are used almost subversively.

Steve de Shazer & Insoo Kim Berg, Milwaukee 2001

The Solution-Focused Essentials

1   The Land of Possibilities

In the solution-focused model, problems only interest us as much as they provide us with clues to the possible solutions. Although problems can be overwhelming, there are always moments when the problem is not there or when the problem is less severe or slightly different than at other times. In other words, there are always exceptions to the problems. These exceptions interest the solution-focused worker because they indicate that there are partial solutions that can be enlarged into broader solutions.

The solution-focused practitioner asks: "What still works in spite of the problems you are facing?" The working hypothesis of the solution-focused approach is that there are always things worth continuing with, that there are always things that still work, and that – in spite of everything – there are always possibilities.

2   The Solution-Focused Image of Man

The Image of Man behind the solution-focused model assumes that:

- Every human being and every human system is fully equipped to cope with life;
- Human systems (individuals, teams, companies, etc.) always have resources at their disposal that they can use to obtain their goals;
- However dire the situation may seem, there are always things that are worthwhile to keep doing;
- There are always things that still work in spite of the problem;
- Change works best on a foundation of what already is there.

3 Resource Orientation

In solution-focused work, one continuously concentrates on the resources the family business members can use to move forward in their (professional) life. A resource can be anything, from your background, intelligence, work, relations, friends, family and environmental factors to convictions, experience, studies (whether or not at the "university of life"), market situations, and so on. Anything can be a resource to draw strength from as long as you make proper use of it. A half-full bottle contains exactly the same reality as a half-empty bottle. Yet, seeing the bottle as half full is a resource that enhances your chance of survival in the desert.

Thinking in terms of resources is so pivotal in the solution-focused approach that it could've just as well been named "resource-focused working."

4 Future Orientation

Solutions belong to the future while problems belong to the past. The solution-focused model offers a wide range of interventions that channel your attention toward constructing possible solutions. Instead of concentrating on the (why of the) problems in the past, the solution-focused model concentrates on the desired outcome: "What do you want to accomplish tomorrow and next week?" "What could be the first little step towards this?"

5 Goal Orientation

The solution-focused approach focuses on the goals of the clients and not on the paradigm that the experts adhere to. In solution-focused work, the only goals that deserve our attention are the goals of the clients, as they need to be aligned with the goals of the family@business. Obviously, the goals of the family@business need to be aligned with normal business best practices, the macro-economic contexts, and the law.

Useful goals are practical, realistic, realizable, can be phrased in behavioral terms ("What will you do different if...") and they preferably go from small to large.

6 Three Mandates

A mandate is the authority required to exercise a function. If we want to regulate traffic at a crossing, we have to make sure that we have a mandate as a police officer. In the perception of the rushing drivers, we are allowed to regulate the traffic because the (hired) uniform makes us look like a police officer. This means you do not "have" a mandate. You "receive" a mandate by earning it from your clients' perspective. A mandate always results from interaction.

As a professional, we always hold three mandates at the same time. We have a leadership mandate that allows us to take the lead in the interventions. We, at the same time, have a management mandate through which we apply our professional knowledge and make agreements with our clients. Our third mandate is our coaching mandate wherein we create a context in which we help the others to help themselves to obtain their goals by making use of their resources.

Solution-focused work means that you have to continuously switch among three mandates. The essence of your mandate as a leader is to know precisely how and when to apply your mandates as a coach or as a manager. After all, it is you who decides – from your expertise, experience, and awareness of the current situation – whether you intervene as a coach or as a manager.

All three mandates are driven by the quality of our working relationship with the clients.

7   Asking questions triumphs over giving statements

Questions help to shape the answers you get and vice versa. Asking appropriate solution-building questions will uncover resources that can be used to build solutions toward the goals of the family and family@ business.

When offering suggestions or even specific directives that stem from your managerial mandate, it is best to phrase those in the form of a question. That way, the client who answers your suggestive question, becomes the owner of the answer, which enhances the chance that the client will actually do it.

8   Minimax decision rules

As a solution-focused professional, we are constantly aiming at obtaining maximal effects with minimal efforts for the clients. In order to reach this minimax effect, you can use the following decision rules:

Rule 1: if something is not broken, do not fix it.
Rule 2: if something is not working, no longer working, or not properly working after trying for a while, then stop, learn from it and do something else.
Rule 3: if something is working well, good enough, or better, just keep doing it and/or do more of it.
Rule 4: if something is working well, good enough, or better, learn it from someone else and/or offer it to someone else.

You can use this list of decision rules as a checklist. Whenever you feel a certain intervention does not work, you can go through this checklist, find what you missed or what you didn't pay enough attention to, and then implement it.

9   Solution Talk

Language is our main instrument. Listening and talking are the main components of "languaging." The cooperation between the professional and his (family@business) clients aims at helping the clients create an alternative reality than their problem state.

Problem Talk: "What is the problem and why?"

Solution Talk: "What still works well in spite of the problem?" "What would you like *instead* of the problem?"

10   The Five-Step Tango

What is it that you actually do in the relationship with your family@business clients? Protocol-driven models follow a fixed script. The solution-focused approach is more like a dance. Since we never know what situations might pop up nor what clients will do or say, it is a far better idea to improvise creative answers that are adapted to the continuously changing and unpredictable conversations. We improvise on a theme that comes from the situation at that moment.

It takes two to tango. In the tango, a minimal number of steps can be combined into endless possible moves between the dance partners.

Solution-focused coaching is like a tango with five basic steps. Each step in the coaching tango is an *activity* to be performed *together with* your client. It starts with making contact (step 1) since the working relationship is the driver for change. After having explored the context (step 2), the client is asked for his goals (step 3), we listen for resources (step 4) and possibilities, and offer relevant compliments (step 5).

The metaphor of the solution tango helps structure and guides the interaction process between yourself and your interlocutors.

The Esthetics of Change

This framework contains a picture of the solution-focused approach as it is painted in broad-brush strokes. The upcoming chapters will detail this picture in the finest possible brush strokes so that the multilayered esthetic gradually will become visible.

In the following chapters, you will encounter all these essentials in the interventions and conversations between the protagonists.

In Chapter 8 (The Solution-Focused Toolkit) the discussions between the family business consultants Mark and Cynthia will reveal details of the solution-focused way of thinking and working. Chapter 9 (The Solution Tango) will show you what to do in the interaction with your family business clients. In Chapter 10 (Conversations with the Siblings) you will see how the solution-focused approach unfolds in the conversations with the family. In Chapter 11 (Next Gen: Eight Tools for Your Future) the individual conversations switch into conversations with the family. Chapter 14 (The Dance of the Stakeholders) invites the management team in the process.

In the coming chapters, you will learn to use the solution-focused model when working with individuals, conducting family conversations, and in team coaching.

Using this framework and the more theoretical explications in the text, you will discover and absorb the intricacies of the solution-focused approach.

The extensive conversations between the protagonists will give you an idea of how it goes in real life, offer you a chance to study the details of the solution focused language and facilitate your in-depth learning.

Chapter 3

Family and Family@business Life Cycle

The Fundamental Challenge in Family@business

When you work with family businesses or when you meet people working in a family business, more often than not the subject of the inseparable tie between family and company is brought up in conversations. The family and the company are continuously, and in turn, each other's fore- and background. The relational dimension in all human systems, in every family structure, in every Family Business is a given. Yet this relational dimension is a challenge. Why?

The reasons for this are simple and obvious:

> Firstly, a Family Business is a unique combination of two different worlds, namely a family and a company. There is a natural tension between these two worlds. Families are supposed to take care of family members while a company is supposed to take care of business. Conflicts can easily arise between the good for the family and the good for the company. Setting clear boundaries while at the same time creating reciprocal beneficial dynamics is the challenge.

> Secondly, most family businesses are driven by strong personalities. When other family members raise issues about the business, these strong personalities can feel criticized and the going can get tough. Developing harmony between all the persons (and different personalities) involved and combining this with a strong leadership is the challenge.

> Thirdly, during a lifetime persons and families on the one hand and companies on the other hand evolve through life cycles. It is a challenge to find the right equilibrium between the different life cycles.

In order to continuously stress this intimate interconnectedness, we will use the neologism "family@business" throughout this book.

DOI: 10.4324/9781003194200-3

Complexity

As time and generations fly by, the structure of a family@business can become very complex.

- Siblings can found a business. Their children can become involved in the company. Some will work there while some will be only shareholders;
- As each generation has more children, the amount of family members in a company can become vast, with all the potential but also with all the space for discord;
- In an extensive family, it happens that the family tree is culled: family members are bought out while others take the lead;
- Family members can start a business with non-family members;
- One family branch has many children while another branch has only one. This has consequences on ownership and leadership that can be far-reaching;
- In Asian countries, it can happen that the Founders have no direct descendants and that someone is adopted for the explicit purpose of continuing the family@business;
- ....

The possibilities are as infinite as the variety between persons, families, and businesses.

For this book, we have chosen the simplest structure. This gives us the opportunity to deconstruct the major dynamics that are common to all possible family structures.

Central Events

Five moments that mark the life of human beings can also be applied to the life of a company.

The *conception*. The conception is the start of human life; and just so, the fundamentals of a company are often laid in a split second of excitement and hope for the future, more precisely the moment in which the decision to start a company is taken. This is probably the most important decision in the endless series of decisions that is called entrepreneurship.

Here everything is charm and excitement; nothing has happened yet, so nothing can go wrong.

The second moment is the *birth*, the actual start that takes place after a period of preparation – the pregnancy as it were. The choices made during this period are often crucial for all further developments. What do I want to do, where do I want to go, with whom do I want to cooperate? For many companies, the problem consists of having had an all too short a pregnancy or none at all. No careful preparation, no clear view of the possibilities and hindrances... Often the problem can be summarized as follows: there is an idea, there is hope but there is no financial plan, no business strategy.

This is the cause for the high death rate among startup companies.

Third moment: *growth*. If the company survives the dangerous first years, there is a good chance that the company will grow in size and complexity. This growth requires a change in the way the company is organized, financed, managed, and led.

What goes up must inevitably come down. The fourth moment is *decline*. People are getting old and companies are getting older. In family@businesses this is an exciting, turbulent, and demanding period. If the company wants to stay alive and evolve into the future, the company's aging founders have to step down gradually, while the younger generation has to step in gradually.

Fifth and last moment: *the end*. Until proven otherwise, all people are mortal. They go through stages of growth, stagnation and decay, and eventually they die. Some companies have a long life, most do not. Companies fail more often than not, miserably; only rarely do they leave the stage gloriously... But those companies that are able to move forward toward a distant future can then grow very old and the leading families become like a kind of dynasty.[1]

Keeping these five central events in mind, we can now proceed to look at things in a more dynamic way.

Intertwining Life Cycles

The development of a family continues through successive phases: family with small children – family with adolescents – children growing up and becoming independent – children leaving the parental home to begin a new cycle, starting with their own "boy meets girl." At that time, the parents often have to take care of their own parents and/or cope with their loss.

Just like the individual and the family moves through their lifecycle, so companies also go through lifecycles. All these stages of life bring their own specific challenges.

There are five phases in the growth of children toward participating in the family@business. All offspring goes through phase 1., but not all children will go through the next stages: some may choose a different path in life instead of becoming active in the family@business. This five-phase model offers a simple yet profound framework. Each phase has its specific challenges for which you will find toolkits in the coming chapters.

You will learn how the life cycle of the family intertwines with the life cycle of the company as you can see in Table 3.1.

Table 3.1 Phases in the Development of the Family/Business

	Phase 1 Birth and Survival	Phase 2 Initial Expansion	Phase 3 Growth toward Complexity	Phase 4 Maturity and Intergenerational Partnership	Phase 5 Power Transfer to Next Gen
Age of Business	0 to 5	5 to 15	15 to 25	25 to 30	30 to 35+
Age of Parents	25 to 35	35 to 50	50 to 60	60 to 65	65 to 70+
Age of Children	0 to 10	10 to 25	25 to 35	35 to ± 45	± 45 to 50
Challenges					
Nature of Business	Struggling for viability	Fast expansion, need to invest time and money	Complex and stable enterprise	Need for strategic "rethinking" and reinvestment	Corporate acceleration
Organizational nature	One-(wo)man business, everybody does everything	Small, dynamic, beginning of teamwork	Professionalization of management	Stagnation/consolidation	Rejuvenated professional business structure and processes
Motivation of Founder-Owner	Carving a niche in the world of business	Concerned with success of business	Business growth	New interests or is "semi retired." The next generation seeks growth and change	Enjoying the successes of G2
Financial expectations for family	Limited to basic necessities	Initial comfort for family	Sponsoring Next Gen's own family steps	Bigger needs, particularly with regard to security and generosity	Enjoying old age in health and luxury
Family objectives	Business success	Work-life balance	Sponsoring Next Gen toward their own households	Family harmony and solidarity	Family harmony and solidarity between (grand)children and extended family

Phase 1: Birth and Survival

Phase I	Age of Business	Age of Parents	Age of Children	Nature of Business	Organizational nature	Motivation of Founder-Owner	Financial Expectations for Family	Family Objectives
Birth and Survival	0 to 5	25 to 35	0 to 10	Struggling for viability	One-(wo)man business, everybody does everything	Carving a niche in the world of business	Limited to basic necessities	Business success

The eternal cycle of generations starts at the magic moment of "boy meets girl" (or vice versa of course). With a bit of luck, a couple will grow out of this meeting, and if a child is born, a family is founded. This family has to maintain itself by working. One possible way to do this is to engage in some sort of independent activity: a one-man business, a company with co-workers, or a partnership in some form or another.

The respective families from which the young couple originates influence the "mental marriage contract" of the newlywed. In the development of a marital relationship, there is often a struggle between two families to determine which of them is being reproduced. The two partners, through their interaction with each other and with the world around them, create the relational interplay of their marriage. They must decide on the appropriate amount of distance they take from their family of origin. They learn the – often unspoken – rules about who does what, about dealing with intimacy, about dealing with income and spending, etc.

Let us assume, in the classic role pattern, that, shortly after their marriage, the couple starts up their own company. The arrival of the first children forces the couple to devote a large amount of their time and energy to the household. The young couple is now confronted with the difficult balance of the two scarcest goods on earth: time and money.

Fact Sheet

Gender in Family Business

The classical male/female role division has been broken, or more precisely, ameliorated in the last decades. In the last 40 years, women increasingly entered the workforce. In many industries, the numbers of women who join the ranks as professionals are rapidly growing. Think about the medical profession, lawyers, bankers, accountants, other financial professions, etc.

The participation of women at the highest level in family businesses is not exempt from this trend.

Yet, this is a trend and there is a long way to go. The numbers in the family business gender studies are not very clear, not definitive, and in some cases not even very useful. Reading all these studies, one has to be careful not to jump to all-too-easy conclusions. When a lobby group that serves a politically correct stance publishes numbers, these numbers can be confusing and downright misleading.

One of the most reliable studies is the 2019 Global Family Business Survey, undertaken by STEP, Successful Transgenerational Entrepreneurship Practices,[2] from which we quote, states:

	Year of birth	Percentage of CEO's still in power	Percentage of female CEO's
Silent generation	1925–1945	7	2
Baby boomers	1945–1964	49	39
Generation X	1965–1980	27	35
Millennials	1981–2000	17	24

Another quote from the same STEP Survey: "The same study shows that 18% of current family business leaders are female, a relatively small percentage suggesting that the 'glass ceiling' at the top remains a challenge." But there is more to quote: "Europe and Asia have 43% of female CEOs, in contrast with North America's where a mere 7% are female CEOs."

From this study, as is the case with most other relevant studies concerning these topics, it is impossible to deduce:

• the percentage of female family Business Foundresses;
• the percentage of women in non-CEO positions that have a major influence on management and strategy of the family@business;
• the influence of women on and in the family@business, even when they do not work in the family firm;
• what happens in the intimacy of the couple where one is on the forefront and the other is highly influential but in the background, etc.

Alternative lifestyles are – luckily – accepted today, for example, the LGTB+ community. Their influence in the dynamics of the family@ business in general is totally unknown. Numbers on these factors are today anecdotal and therefore only relevant to the individuals and individual families involved.

The bad news, when one delves into gender studies and their relevance for the family@business, is that we enter a confusing forest of numbers that limits and even prevents us to see the individual (family) tree. Yet, we consider these changes as important steps forward because the diversity of partnerships and therefore of new and creative ways of developing businesses, opens an unchartered new world of possibilities.

There is however also good news. Whatever the constellation of the family that co-creates a family@business, the family dynamics in general are rather similar. Only the particulars differ from person to person, from family to family, from business to business, and even from moment to moment.

Therefore we dare to kindly ask our readers, permission for the traditional description of the male/female role distribution, especially in the Founding generation or G1. We invite you to read the "he/she" with your own family composition in mind. For the sake of readability, we do not use he/she but just he or she.

From birth till the moment children become involved in the family@ business, they have a tangential relationship with the business. Depending on the situation, there comes a moment when children become aware that their parents have a special job, different from most of the other kids' parents. They slowly learn to appreciate that the company their parents work in, is like a family member: important, always there, time- and energy-consuming. The challenge for the parents is to find a life-work balance and show the children that they come first. At the same time, it is crucial that the children learn to respect and love their "eldest sibling." To realize this, parents need to have an optimistic view on the company and share their love of the company with the kids. The parenting cares the children receive will help them become self-reliant individuals and this is the foundation upon which a further education can be grafted. This crucial phase creates a context in which children can develop into well-balanced persons and is a launching pad toward their possible participation in the family@business.

The newly created company is – of course – a fragile little creature, which demands a great deal of effort, time, energy, and devotion, just like a newborn child.

John and Annie

Once the software package was ready, sales followed rapidly. Annie took care of processing orders, payments, and all financial matters. She became the homebound nave in the wheel of success of the young company. John became the flying warrior, spending more time in hotels visiting clients, prospects, and international conferences. He created the software program by writing source code that could be adapted for use in all kinds of construction projects all over the world. John always had an upscale in mind. He thinks big. Annie designed an organizational structure that could cope with their dreams for the future. Besides being a couple and parents, they became co-entrepreneurs.

Within two years they had to move the business out of the apartment. That necessitated travel time to work, adding extra organization for the family and less time for the kids.

In between, little Ella was born.

Startup companies tend to have high operational costs and low profits while the turnover is rather modest and still unpredictable.

For practical and financial reasons, the young family often lives on the premises of the company. Father devotes all his time and energy to the company, while mother is supposed to take on the households' tasks and the raising of the young children. Although both live and work in the same building, there is nonetheless little contact between them: both are completely absorbed by their respective tasks. Usually, the mother helps in the office: secretary work, the reception of customers, administrative tasks, bookkeeping, etc. Her (free) help is a big financial advantage for the young company. Apart from the occasional "quality-time" with the kids, father devotes his energy exclusively to their eldest child, the company. Being constantly together while at the same time being absorbed in totally separated activities, the young couple now has to be careful that they do not drift apart. Emotional problems emerge out of this closeness-separation and can have negative consequences both to their life as a couple and to their entrepreneurial enthusiasm. The marital challenge is to find the right balance.

平衡

Pínghéng

The personality of the Founder[3] is of great importance. As the driving force of the company, he takes all the decisions and assumes all the economical responsibilities. Founders often are more "Do-ers" than "Thinkers." When starting the company, the Founder had to do almost everything by himself. He tends to lose himself in the idea that "if you don't do things yourself, they are not done well." Later on, some Founders keep doing things by themselves because they are convinced that instead of explaining to others how they want things to be done, it's faster to do it themselves. Founders tend to limit the delegation of tasks to just giving orders. In small startup companies where just a few employees work and people have no experience, it is not easy to know who is best in what tasks, what is the best way to handle things, how to solve the problems that arise every day. In this stage, they have to learn by experience, by trial and error, and sometimes one has to learn lessons the hard way. The boss has to learn what it means to be the boss, what it means to cooperate, how to handle differences between his employees, how to handle conflicts, etc. In general, job descriptions are not available, and if they exist, they are very vague and offer not much of a guideline. In such an environment, it is the personality of the Founder that makes the difference. Unfortunately, some Founders stick to this way of managing their company even when it grows into a much bigger corporation.

Phase 2: Initial Expansion by Founder-Manager

Phase 2	Age of Business	Age of Parents	Age of Children	Nature of Business	Organizational Nature	Motivation of Founder-Owner	Financial expectations for family	Family objectives
Initial expansion	5 to 15	35 to 50	10 to 25	Fast expansion, need to invest time and money	Small, dynamic, beginning of teamwork	Concerned with success of business	Initial comfort for family	Work-life balance

Mother and/or father are the only members of the household involved in the business. Aside from an occasional little job during vacations or going with their parents to the office on Sunday mornings, the children are not involved in the business. The family develops, the business develops, and all individuals develop. School and education is central for the children. The entrepreneurial parents help their business surf the waves of growth. The first (non-) family employees are invited to join. The complexity of the business grows. At the same time, the children go through an important and challenging phase called puberty, a.k.a hormonal storm time. Family ties come under strain and all involved need their uttermost cool to safely surf on the turbulent waves of personal growth.

Coping with the children's puberty is like walking a tightrope with a side wind of the force of a hurricane. Coping with this phase in the company's turbulence is a very similar exercise.

John and Annie

John and Annie did a great job. Not only were they successful in building their little startup into a leading software company, with their youngest child Cherly born, they also created a family with three children. A young as they were at that time, the kids realized that something special was going on. John stayed passionate about his code writing and developed himself into a successful entrepreneur. Annie soon had to say goodbye to her accounting job to become the formal CFO in the family@business.

As the young company grows, more employees are coming to work in its dynamic team. Trustworthiness and loyalty to the company are important values: one has to be able to count on each other.

Sometimes this is translated as: the employees are supposed to support the personal goals of the Founder. If these goals are business oriented, that is not a problem. But if these goals are just personal, this Founder will not go very far with his new company and he will not be able to retain valuable employees.

The organization in young companies often is very informal. Non-family employees are more or less considered as non-family family: the non-family manager spends so much time and energy on a shared dream with the Founder that very intensive relationships are likely to develop.

If the company survives this start-up phase, it comes in the second stage, where it is confronted with growing pains. This can happen relatively soon after the first successes, when the company starts operating at cruising speed.

John and Annie

The first collaborator they hired was John's lifelong friend Bert, a non-nerdy programmer with a big social life. Soon Alice followed. Trained as a language teacher and fascinated with marketing, she started the website, all company brochures, and prepared the presentations for John's visits and talks. This small team formed the base for the rapid growth of the company, both in terms of revenue and in terms of personnel. Before long, the startup morphed into a powerhouse in its niche. At the 10th birthday celebration of the founding of the company, over 100 employees were at the party.

Control over what happens and individual performance are not considered the most important management issues in this stage. Everybody involved in the young company is focused on short-term business successes.

Overlapping Systems

The overlap of the two systems, i.e. family-business, creates a natural spillover between the two systems: e.g. family roles spill over to the business and business rules spill over to the family. This spillover does not have to be detrimental if the family's pattern of functioning supports sound business management and vice versa.

Beware of Role Confusion

One of the dangers for a family@business is a phenomenon called role confusion. This means that someone confuses the role he or she has in one system with his or her role in the other system. Role confusion is detrimental to both family harmony and business results.

Classic examples:

•   In classic gender terms (which fortunately age quickly and the classical gender terms might soon become obsolete), father is the CEO at work and behaves in the same way at home. Mother is the CEO at home (CEO means Chief Emotional Officer) and in the office she behaves in the same way with the result that some employees abuse her attitude. (Or vice versa, obviously)

- The youngest child, who is spoiled at home, behaves like a spoiled brat at the office.
- The Foundress, used at being the boss and giving orders to people, comes home at night and orders family members around there too. These family members may not readily accept this.

How to deal with role confusion?

- Make a clear distinction between family life and work, so that everyone unites around the hard work that a family@business requires. In short: "separate in order to unite better and unite in order to separate better." This will make it easier to separate the two worlds while they remain united.
- A clear perception of and an open attitude to this counter-productive transfer of acts from private to professional life, and vice versa, prevents this role of confusion from becoming a bad habit. Because role confusion occurs unconsciously, it only becomes apparent when it causes serious problems in business and/or family matters. As a result, the awareness that this phenomenon exists makes preventive action possible.
- If the phenomenon of role confusion pops up, it can be solved by open communication and accordingly changing the behavior that comes with it.

John and Annie

By now, Eric, 20, is in his second year at the university. Ella, 15, works hard at school because she is adamant she wants to prepare for medical school. The youngest daughter Cherly is 12 and begins her time in high school. Although very different personalities, the children agree on one thing: "Mom and Dad

Phase 3: Growth toward Complexity

Phase 3	Age of Business	Age of Parents	Age of Children	Nature of Business	Organizational nature	Motivation of Founder-Owner	Financial Expectations for Family	Family Objectives
Growth toward Complexity	15 to 25	50 to 60	25 to 35	Complex and stable enterprise	Professionalization of management	Business growth	Sponsoring Next Gen's own family steps	Sponsoring Next Gen toward their own households

did a great job. We haven't seen them too much when we were young, but hey, whenever it was really important, they were there for us."

During the first stage, the company had mainly been the Founder's playground. Now it is growing fast and this growth often is due to the involvement of the employees. This implies growth in turnover, growth in personnel, more and more complex products, an expanding client network, and additional investments. The organization becomes more complex.

The company, in a manner of speaking, starts leading its own life.

The purely economic necessities that now push the company on can be different from the needs and wishes of the founder!

The Founder no longer has the same general overview of all the details of this company. Often Founders in this stage say: "it is growing over my head." Some Founders have a hard time to cope with this third phase. They have to adapt their management style to the new situation. Management by control is no longer possible or useful. Not everybody has the necessary flexibility to make this transition. If the Founder is not able or willing to do so, he/she can become a bottleneck for the development of the organization.

In this phase, the Founder must delegate many tasks, allow others to take over vital functions in the company and he must be able to hand over the power of decision to others, be it family members, be it non-family employees.

As a matter of fact, this is the transition from a one-person business to a real family business, in which other members of the (non-family) family have a growing influence on the way the business is run. The founder must be prepared to gradually let go of his direct influence in exchange for indirect influence through his leadership. Plan-Do-Check-Adjust must become Plan-Do-Trust.

This transition of a company led by an individual to a Family Business can take up quite some time. To discuss this openly and to take the time to write down a business strategy takes time and courage. The Founder needs to look into the crystal ball of the future and this can be confrontational, hence courage is needed.

John and Annie

For some years, John and Annie have treated themselves twice a year to a weekend away from home and business. It started out as a small vacation, but they soon realized that it gave them time to reconnect as a couple. Passionate about their eldest child, the family@business, they started prolonging these weekends into a weeklong retreat in which they discussed business strategy and made plans for the future. It became a habit that their closest collaborators – their non-family family as they called them –

were invited for the second half of that week to share, fine-tune, and hone those plans.

One of the results was that they decided to expand the family@business from a software company into an actual construction company. *"When we claim to have the most comprehensive software package to facilitate the construction business, why not use it ourselves as proof by diversifying into construction?"* Their sales department, who immediately showed them that the clients would see them as competitors, killed this idea. They changed tactics and let their clients built for them, using their software. That way they created a solid portfolio of buildings, first for their own use as offices in the different countries and later on, just as an investment. After 15 years of this strategy, they had a real estate portfolio that was bigger as a company than the software part, although – big smile from John – not as profitable.

The Company: Solution Builders International

By now, the business has grown into several companies and in several countries. The original software company keeps expanding according to the chosen strategy where cooperation with construction and investment companies offers the best of both worlds. Their software is rapidly becoming a standard, which means more internationalization. Their real estate portfolio diversifies from office building into hotels, schools, and hospitals. Most of the profit in the first 15 years is ploughed back into the companies so that dependence on the banks becomes lesser over the years. The solid reputation of Solution Builders International brings all kinds of business proposals. An investment manager is needed and that team grows with the rest of the company.

Twenty years after John slammed the door shut on his employer, their company is financially sound and secure. It has grown into an organization with several business units that each needs a manager, several subsidiaries in different countries that each needs a country manager, a staff organization in headquarters that comprises financial, legal, human resources, marketing, and investment management that needs a general manager. Add the employees in operations and the total adds up to 375 people working in John and Annie's companies.

Business opportunities like a golf club, a chain of fitness clubs, and resorts land on John's desk. With the help of his investment team, John studies the offers and chooses which to follow through. Annie still supervises all of finances while John in his role as CEO is like a fish in the water.

That doesn't mean it has always been a walk in the park. Tough decisions needed to be taken, hurting people. When a big client went broke, a heavy financial burden shook the company. It took Olympic efforts and many sleepless nights to overcome this. Yet, lessons were learned.

While the founder is confronted with the economic challenges and risks, as well as with the necessity of growth, it is not clear whether his children are actually interested in the company, let alone whether they will have the qualities necessary to stand their ground in the company.

John and Annie

The eldest son, Eric, became an engineer like his father and, after some jobs abroad, mostly in multinational companies, he joined the family business. He is on the fast track to a managerial position.

Ella was born after her parents jumped into the deep end by founding their business. She takes no part in the family business. She is following her life dream of becoming a medical doctor.

Cherly who is the youngest has doubts about her studies and claims that she is not ready to choose a career: "I want to travel the world." Nothing came out of this. She planned a yearlong tour of Asia but was home after three weeks. After a year of rebellion, she was coerced into doing something constructive with her life and she started studying marketing. She never finished this but joined the company as a secretary to Alice, the marketing manager and confidante of her parents.

The business-owning parents have to find a balance between allowing their children to find their own way in life (even if it leads them away from the family business) and preparing them for a life in business. It is normal that the Founders hope that their children show interest in the business. It is tempting to push them toward the business. It is extremely difficult to keep an objective view on one's own children when it comes to their business capabilities.

In this phase, the company can only keep growing by allowing more and more non-family members to participate. The non-family members working in a Family Business need special attention. Very often, non-family members have been involved in the company right from the start. The growth of the business and the fact that the members of the family, by virtue of their blood ties, usually occupy a special position, can lead to precarious situations. Status in the company, prospects of promotion, prospects of financial rewards, and the special relationships between the members of the family; they are all aspects that have to be thoroughly controlled to prevent the demotivation or even the loss of these non-family employees. Non-family employees deserve good career planning and the Founder has an important task in this. His biggest challenge now is Leadership.

When the children grow up, some of them will probably work in the Family Business while other siblings blaze their own trail outside the Family Business realm.

When the Family Business enters this Phase 3, the children have received both their parental education as well as the major part of their school education.

Worldwide all Family Business specialists recommend that the ideal career path for Next Gen is to first start working for other companies in order to gain experience in a more neutral context. Some Family@business even make this a requirement before admitting Next Gen to their own Family Business. The main argument is that Next Gen needs to build some track record in order to acquire credibility and develop a greater mandate as a future leader. This is correct but not always possible because it depends on the specific vicissitudes in life: sudden, unexpected, and unprepared grave illness or even death of the Founder, a business opportunity or calamity whereby the Next Gen is needed in the management, an unforeseen or unpredictable possibility for a take-over, a hostile bid on the company by a competitor, ...

At whatever time the Next Gen enters the Family Business, it is the task of the Founding Generation to create a clear, challenging, and safe context in which the Next Gen's management and leadership skills can be developed, trained, and honed.

John and Annie

Seeing that Eric was successful in different companies, John and Annie invite him to join the family@business. He works himself up from intern over blue-collar toward white-collar jobs and functions. In order to learn the business, Eric passes through all divisions, from operations through logistic to manufacturing through administration. And then he moves toward product development, marketing, finance, HR, and finally in a higher management position. He develops trust in himself, trust in the company, and gradually earns the trust of the employees. His parents, the owner-founders, witness and enjoy their son's professional growth. The foundation for transfer/takeover is laid.

The way the second generation enters the Family Business is important. In the literature on this topic, you can read that it is preferable that the children prepare their business career outside the family business. This is indeed the best scenario but it happens relatively seldom.

A smart way to help them integrate in the Family Business is to invite a trusted non-family manager to supervise this process. There are several advantages to this: it gives the non-family manager an important job and proves to him that his competence is appreciated, the founder learns how to delegate this task, the emotional conflicts caused by the role confusion of mother and son versus boss and co-worker are thus avoided. The ideal is that the family members are trained according to an objective strategic plan, rather than receiving a position in the company for the sole reason of bearing the name of the founder. Otherwise, you run the risk that the "fils-à-papa" syndrome will emerge.

As the business "matures" and its Founder grows older, the business is fully developed. The company is likely to have subsidiaries, semi-independent business daughters, several plants at different locations, and even international ventures. Non-family managers and executives are in high positions.

Phase 4: Maturity and Intergenerational Partnership

Phase 4	Age of Business	Age of Parents	Age of Children	Nature of Business	Organizational Nature	Motivation of Founder-Owner	Financial Expectations for Family	Family Objectives
Maturity and Intergenerational partnership	25 to 30	60 to 65	35 to ±45	Need for strategic "rethinking" and reinvestment	Stagnation/consolidation	New interests or is "semi retired." The next generation seeks growth and change	Bigger needs, particularly with regard to security and generosity	Family harmony and solidarity

A management team is needed to keep the oversight of all operations and steer the complex business system through the waves and turbulences of the market. Business wise, the Founder's interest has shifted from daily operations to more strategic issues. The Founders also enter a next stage in their personal life cycle and other things than just work (slowly) become more important: grandchildren, harmony in the family, charity and other meaningful and meaning-giving activities, preparing for old age, ...

At this stage, in most family@businessses, the next generation has taken over some of the leadership and they have important functions in the company. If all goes well, the Founding generation begins to gradually shift ownership toward the next generation. This is a delicate balancing act of giving and deserving trust between G1 and G2.

Given that neither G1 nor G2 has any experience with this process, it is best to take one's time and accept help from more experienced partners, be it consultants, coaches, or friends-colleagues businessmen who have been through the transfer process. Now the sensibilities of all stakeholders, including non-family staff and family members who will not participate in the future business must be considered. Patience and persistence are vital in this phase since this transfer defines future success.

Gradually G1 invites G2 to become more and more of a business partner. Founder and next generation share not only a percentage of ownership, but they also start to share the leadership of the company. As time goes by and both parties experience growing trust in the path chosen, the share of the Next Gen grows steadily. It develops into a partnership that prepares the fading out of the Founding generation.

This is a challenging period, both in the personal and family lives of the people involved as well as in the business sides of the matter. From a personal perspective, the Founder needs to learn that he no longer coincides with the business. The Next Gen is confronted with a less comfortable position than in the years they were learning the business and could operate from the sideline, without having to take the full responsibility. Family-wise, Father and Next Gen have to learn to become business partners and that implies the development of a totally different relationship style than just the family relationship. On top of that, if there are other children, the relationship with and between the children, active and non-active in the company, needs adaptation.

Business wise, difficult choices have to be taken one after the other: expanding or consolidating; diversification or not; cooperating with external partners or continuing to play solo; retaining financial autonomy or admitting external capital; staying privately held or becoming a listed company, etc. Companies in this phase often need a strategic reorientation and large reinvestment projects because they have been running at cruise speed for some years. This puts an extra financial strain on the next generation who need to make long-term financial decisions at a moment when they are not yet (or maybe just becoming) the owners of the company.

Two key elements are simultaneously important in this phase: the ownership succession is interwoven with the management succession. These elements make this phase complicated both from the family as well as from the business perspective. Business wise, the Next Gen needs to take the lead in the management succession in order to show all stakeholders, Founders included, that they have the strengths and capabilities to become the leaders for the future. This is the moment that the Next Gen structures the management of the company according to their hopes and beliefs. This is the moment that the Next Gen earns the respect of all stakeholders and lays the foundations for all collegial relationships in their coming "reign."

At the same time, the family needs to plan the ownership succession. The founding generation needs to think about the way they will organize their inheritance.

The fair distribution of the wealth among all the children in such a way that the continuation of the company is not endangered is a difficult and complex task. By this time there are often in-laws and grandchildren involved, and neither will all the children be involved in the company to the same degree.

All these aspects make it necessary for the ownership and management succession to be tailor-made. This process is (better: must be) as unique as the family and the company themselves.

John and Annie

Over the years, Eric went through many jobs and many functions within the family@business. In the beginning, he worked as an engineer in operations. After a while, he worked abroad as a country manager. In that period he struggled with his personal life. Eventually, he took the courage to admit to himself and to his parents that he was homosexual. After a little shock, John and Annie made it clear that this wouldn't change their love for him. They immediately accepted his friend Lars. From then on, Eric took responsibilities in almost all departments from finance to sales, from business development to Mergers & Acquisitions. By showing his leadership capabilities, he earned respect and trust both within the company as with external stakeholders. By now, Eric is the CEO. Although working long hours, Eric is a family man. He cherishes his husband Lars and their adopted children, Esther and John Jr.

John took the time to coach Eric into his current role. At first, they both went to the meetings with the banks, larger clients, and other strategically important stakeholders. They share a secretary and a personal assistant who work in an office that is located between John and Eric's offices. Both Eric and John put a lot of time and effort in coaching their top managers. Together they managed an important reorganization project to prevent the company from stagnation. Once the new organizational structure was in place, John gradually stepped back. He started by delegating many of his tasks to the staff he trusts and by inviting Eric to take over the supervisory role. Lately, John only works from Tuesday till Thursday.

Annie withdrew from the management team and is only present during the quarterly meetings of the board of directors. She is helpful with the grandchildren. She spends a lot of time and energy in charity work.

Cherly works her way up in the marketing department. Eric invited her recently to join the management team. Her parents are a little worried that she still is single.

Ella became an urologist and lives together with her longtime partner Max.

Phase 5: Power Transfer to Next Gen

Phase 5	Age of Business	Age of Parents	Age of Children	Nature of Business	Organizational Nature	Motivation of Founder-Owner	Financial Expectations for Family	Family Objectives
Power transfer to Next Gen	30 to 35+	65 to 70+	± 45 to 50	Corporate acceleration	Rejuvenated professional business structure and processes	Enjoying the successes of G2	Enjoying old age in health and luxury	Family harmony and solidarity between (grand) children and extended family

This whole process of transfer to each Next Generation is a dance between both transferor and transferee. The opening passes are set in the parent-child relationship. The dance ends when the partners break apart and each find a new role in personal and business life. Then the parent-child relationship remains in the business family, while the professional roles become completely different in the family@business.

With the transferal of ownership and leadership now realized, the Next Gen assumes full control and all final responsibilities. Now the Founders sit in the backseat and enjoy the ride. Only when asked for, they enjoy their role as coach and share their business experience happily with the company.

Future Generations

The Next Gen starts its own family@business life cycle, only from a more complex business starting point. If the Next Gen succeeds in repeating the same cycle and brings the family@business into the third generation, then with luck, hard work, and devotion to the long term, the foundation is there for the Family Business to become a dynasty.

John and Annie

They enjoy a life of leisure, surrounded by their grandchildren. The family regularly comes together for dinners. John gave up his office. Some of the new employees don't even recognize him when he stops by in the head-quarters office to say hello. John and Annie are delighted by the successes of their children and appreciate the way they safeguard the future of the family@business.

Conclusion

Understanding and respecting the interconnectedness between family life cycle and company life cycle creates the platform for future.

All individual and family versus company life cycles are interwoven. The challenge is to create an intertwinement like two climbing roses that grow together around the tree of life.

Notes

1 There exists an international association of Bicentenary Family Companies, called The Henokiens (www.henokiens.com). Membership to the Henokiens Association is based on company longevity (the minimum period of existence is 200 years) and permanence (the family must be owner or majority shareholder of the company and one member of the founding family must still manage the company or be a member of the board). Furthermore, the company must be in good financial health and up to date.
2 This study won the 2020 FFI Achievement Award, www.digital.ffi.org
3 As said, these role patterns are changing. So, the term "foundress" can easily replace the term "founder." Again, family dynamics are generally similar, while in each person, each couple, each family, and each family@business case the dynamics are unique.

Chapter 4

Education Is the Mother of Leadership

John and Annie

Neither John nor Annie comes from a business background. Both their fathers were blue-collar workers and – coincidentally – both their mothers were nurses. Both fathers had a second job. But their parents were adamant that their children got a better life. They all put great value on the education of their children. In order to be able to pay for university, they set aside every possible penny. John and Annie got that chance, but they also knew that they had to produce good scholarly results because failure was not an option.

Even before John and Annie expanded their business, they discussed what consequences their venture would have on their personal life, their marriage, and their family. They decided that whatever happened in their working life, they would always give priority to the education of the kids, even if that meant that some business deals had to be postponed or canceled.

Education Is an Offer

In childhood and youth, by example, parents can instill a culture of respect, resilience, hard work, responsibility, self-care, honesty, the art of taking small steps toward betterment of oneself, the joy of obtaining results both in school as among friends as in personal ventures (sports, music, the arts).

Offering an education to your children is maybe your grandest task in life. This task can feel overwhelmingly difficult, prone to failure, and stressful. Therefore, it can be soothing to keep the following in mind: you can't educate children since they can only educate themselves. Education is an offer. The only thing you can (and must) do is to create a loving, open, and safe environment that enhances the chances that your children accept this offer of education and make the best of it for them. Remember: you can lead the horse to the water, make sure the water is safe to drink but you can't force the horse to drink.

DOI: 10.4324/9781003194200-4

Age-Appropriate MUST-DO's

If you, as an educator, want to achieve the best possible educational result for your children, then it is advisable to act in an age-adequate manner. The following list shows you which pedagogical interventions are suitable for the age group in question. The age indications are of course averages. It is advisable to take into account that each child is different so that you can fine-tune your pedagogical interventions accordingly.

- 0–5 years: Safety, warmth and security, fun and love (also useful for all ages and in dealing with yourself and all other people).
- 5–10 years: Small responsibilities, sharing, delaying of gratification, introduce the business side in a playful manner to the children. Play is more important than results yet play also needs persistence/perseverance, concentration, dealing with frustration, resilience, and focus.
- 10–14 years: Bigger responsibilities, first meeting with FB in terms of little visits and work there, delaying gratification for longer time, do not hide problems/difficulties but show that there is always a solution. Importance of school and learning but also of reaching out to others (communication and relationship skills are best internalized in this age)
- 14–20 years: Gradually bigger and bigger participation in the com-munication, knowledge, appreciation, problem-solving skills that come with being part of a family@business. Invite to work in FB under tutelage of well-meaning non-family preferably from down on the corporate ladder. Give doable but significant responsibilities for jobs and let this responsibility grow following previous successes. Mind you: dealing positively with mistakes is in itself a success! School is important, learning with open mind is more important. Encourage interest outside of the family@business so that the Mind opens like a parachute. Learning-to-learn is top priority. Enhance Emotional Intelligence by parental example. Demonstrate by example the vital values of respect for and ethics toward others. Allow to fly solo. During a big part of this age period, the person undergoes major hormonal, bio- and psychological changes called puberty. Puberty is like a river: don't push it but embed it in safe banks so it can't flashflood.
- Especially during puberty and adolescence, it is of utmost importance that the individual finds its own identity. The parents need to allow and even support this process of individuation, even if it can cause a turbulent time for the family.
- 20–30 years Young adults: Next Generation enters "real" life, both in their personal life (first steady partner, choosing and ending formal education and training) as in professional life.

• 30 years till death: Adult life where the following values are relevant: guidance from more experienced elders, learning zeal, humbleness, hard and smart work, vision and adaptability, preparing your next generation, and accepting the cycle of (business) life.

The Power of Delayed Gratification

Walter Mischel, a professor of psychology, discovered in the late 60s, that the ability to delay gratification as a child greatly predicts how one functions in later life. When under great situational pressures and confronted with "hot temptations," little children who are able to suppress their need for immediate gratification and wait for a greater reward, show the extremely important resource of being able to use self-control.

His work became known as "the Marshmallow test" of which you can see impressive and at the same time hilarious examples on YouTube. How did he test this? He seated preschool children alone at a table and presented them with a desired treat, in this case a marshmallow. Before leaving the room, he presented the children a choice: to eat the marshmallow or wait until I come back and be rewarded with two marshmallows. While some children were unable to wait even one full minute ("low delayers"), others were able to wait up to 20 minutes ("high delayers") by employing various distraction techniques (e.g. singing, looking at the walls and ceiling, turning around in their chairs, hands over their eyes, etc). In long-term follow-up studies, Mischel discovered that the "high delayers" achieved greater academic success, had better health (e.g. less substance abuse), more positive relationships (e.g. lower divorce rates), and higher average incomes in later working life. There are no data yet what this might mean for family@business "high delayers" (this is an invitation for Ph.D candidates!!) but there is no reason to suppose there is a difference. These longtime results show that being able to delay immediate satisfaction (one marshmallow) by using self-control to get a deferred but more desirable outcome (two marshmallows) is an important resource in life. Furthermore, Mischel and his team discovered that if they taught the children some mental tricks – such as pretending that the marshmallow is only a picture or a cloud, it became much easier to delay. This implies that the resource of delaying gratification is not a fixed trait but it is a resource that can be trained. Mischel testifies: "Once you realize that willpower is just a matter of learning how to control your attention and thoughts, you can really begin to increase it. This task forces kids to find a way to make the situation work for them. They want the second marshmallow, but how can they get it? We can't control the world, but we can control how we think about it and therefore we can control our actions." (SOURCE: https://www.newyorker.com/magazine/2009/05/18/dont-2)

Obviously it's not enough just to teach kids mental tricks – the real challenge is turning those tricks into habits, and that requires years of diligent practice. "This is where your parents are important," Mischel says. "Have they established rituals that force you to delay on a daily basis? Do they encourage you to wait? And do they make waiting worthwhile?" According to Mischel, even the most mundane routines of childhood – such as not snacking before dinner, or saving up your allowance, or holding out until Christmas morning – are really sly exercises in cognitive training: we're teaching ourselves how to think so that we can outsmart our desires.

Success usually comes down to choosing the pain of discipline over the ease of immediate satisfaction.

It is obvious that a lifelong training in delayed gratification will serve the children well in their later personal and family@business life. Family@business is all about working toward future goals while not being distracted by short-term seductions.

MUST-NOT-DO's for All Ages

Raising children is one of the most difficult tasks we face in our lives. Because each child's upbringing is different, there is little experience to be gained and it is always a "single case design." Therefore, knowing what to avoid is as important as knowing what to do.

- Do not allow a drive for results to stifle your children's right to a playful childhood;
- Do not create an atmosphere of anxiety and distrust in the future;
- Do not show fake optimism;
- Do not isolate your children from the inevitable hardships of life, as this will prevent them from building resilience;
- Do not frenetically try to hide all your problems, fears, and even marital tensions as if they were holy secrets or taboos that you shouldn't share (your children already know them anyway);
- Do not make the family@business off-limits by telling G+ how utterly difficult and hard business life is;

- Do not make working in the family@business the only option thinkable and acceptable;
- Do not deliver immediate gratification for the only reason that "I love my children and I want them to have the best, especially after all I've missed myself";
- Do not talk about business, and certainly not about your family@ business as a dangerous jungle where everybody is up against you.

(Joke: if you want to scare your children away from the family@business, do exactly the opposites)

TEN BEST PRACTICES for Preparing Your Next Generation

When your children reach the age of young adults, or sometimes even earlier, and they indicate an interest in the family@business, it is time to prepare them for life in business. The following interventions have proven to be useful.

1. Start as early as possible:
    Learning leadership skills takes time, effort, and trial and error. So, encourage your children to start early. It is wise to help your children start early. Encourage them to participate in situations where they can gain leadership experiences. This can be at school, in team sports, in scouting, on summer camp, ... Later on, support them when they want to participate – and preferably take up a leadership role – in sororities or fraternities, debating clubs, charity ventures, ...If they are inclined to do so, allow them to make the vacation schedule for the family, to coordinate the planning of family reunions, ...
2. Clarify the norms and values of both your family and the business:
    Every person has totally unique fingerprints. The same goes for families. The same goes for companies and the same goes for a family@ business in dealing with the complexities of family and business systems.
    In your daily life, your values shine through in what you think, what you do, how you do it, how you interact with others, and how you feel about issues. By making your values explicit, you automatically create the standards that guide your life and work. In order to be the best possible role model for their children, it is necessary that the Founding Generation is aware of the norms and values they live by. In a Family@business it is useful to make them explicit, write them down so that they can be beacons for everybody. These norms and values will – obviously – have influence on their business manners.
    Norms and values evolve over time and adapt to changing circumstances. But your core values often span a lifetime. It makes your business

decisions and actions more predictable, transparent, and synchronous with whom you are as a person and as a family as you can see in the next figure.

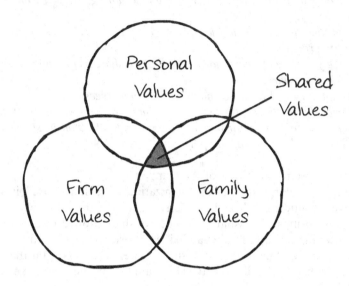

When this is clear, you only have to do what you say and say what you do. That way, the Founding Generation enacts their norms and values and become a role model. The words of the successor of Howard Schultz, the founder of Starbucks, after Howard stepped down as CEO, illustrate this: "My job is to help transition Starbucks from a leader-led company into a leader inspired company." (Financial Times December 10, 2018 on plane to Shanghai).

The same challenge goes for every family@business Next Gen.

John and Annie

Annie: *Both our mothers were nurses. They taught us the value of caring for people. The more care you give, the more you get in return.*

John: *I recognize this from my mother, who also was a nurse. Caring however never meant patronizing.*

Annie: *On the contrary, they cared for us so that we would take care of ourselves. Our parents taught us to share with others.*

John: *Although none of our parents were entrepreneurs, they showed us to dare in life. I remember my father challenging me to sing a song for a large audience when I was about nine years old. I was scared to death,*

> but he supported me. It was a success; he enjoyed my success and I
> myself enjoyed it.

Annie: Luckily you no longer sing these days. (Laughs)

John: Daring was a big value but also realistic daring, not overconfident
daredevilry.

Annie: My father always told us kids: "reach for the moon but keep your feet
on the ground."

John: There you have our personal values that we share as a family: caring,
sharing and daring.

Annie: We also try to live those values for our employees.

John: Obviously we allow everybody to develop his or her own values. When
you want to work with and work for our family@business, shared
values are the best starting point.

3. Share the collective ambition of the company:

A company, corporation, or organization's "raison d'être" is the
collective ambition of all stakeholders, Next Gen included: who and
what do we want to be, what values do we share, how do we want to
create meaning on top of value-added? In short: what makes us tick?

This Collective Ambition as a business driver is so important that we
will deal with it in detail later. (CH17. Family@business Management
Tools)

For now, it suffices to state that when the time is right – remember
age appropriateness – you invite your Next Gen to first take notice of
and later immerse themselves in the consequences of this collective
ambition. Teenagers often are more interested in meaning than in
money and this is a window of opportunity to involve them.

Ask your Next Gen what they think the Collective Ambition of the
company is, what elements they would like to stress and/or add. Invite
them to sit in on organizational discussions about this theme. Invite them
as participants in the yearly review board. In short, involve them.

4. Give the Next Gen real jobs with real responsibilities:

The employees learn to know them as children when they do their first
little jobs during vacations. After their studies and sometimes after they
have done a tour of duty in other companies, they typically start at the
bottom of the corporate ladder. It is important that the Next Gen, from
their very first little vacation job to their entrance position in the "real"
work, get job assignments with real responsibility. There is nothing as
mind numbing as work that does not involve any responsibility.

Next-generation leaders need opportunities to make ever more
complex decisions and experience the results of those decisions. That
way they enter into a constructive feedback loop.

For the rest it works like in sports: start slow, pick up speed while you
learn and persist.

5. Replenish responsibility with accountability:

First give your Next Gen responsibility for tasks and make them – as soon as possible – also accountable for both the work process and for the results. True entrepreneurship is the combination of being responsible and being accountable. E.g. if you give them the leadership of a small department, then your Next Gen must take responsibility for how his/her team functions, including the team's results. Making them accountable for the results is one step further because they reap the profits of good results and "suffer" the consequences when the results are bad.

Remember, that this is a learning process that requires a delicate build up. You want to avoid overzealousness that comes with the risk of burnout. Asking trusted non-family leaders to provide accurate feedback on the Next Gen's performance often is a good tool in this phase. That way, you and your Next Gen create a safe context in which both slowly learn to differentiate the parental-child role from the Boss-employee role.

6. Emotional intelligence (EQ) tops over business ingenuity:

Although it is obvious that one must know his business and one must how business in general operates, knowing how to deal with others combined with knowing how to deal with oneself defines business success.

EQ is another way of being smart. EQ is the ability to identify, use, understand, and manage your own emotions in positive ways to relieve stress, communicate effectively, empathize with others, overcome challenges, and defuse conflict to effectively handle relationships.

While IQ has a large genetic basis and is more nature than nurture, EQ is more nurture than nature and thus can be honed.

It is helpful to teach the Next Gen the power of using their EQ. Giving them feedback and using post-mortem discussions after emotional meetings, helps their awareness so that they become sensitive to their emotions, regulate them appropriately, and learn to avoid impulsive negative emotion-based reactions. Teaching them to become ever more aware of the other's emotional makeup enhances empathy and creates constructive relationship that proves to be much more successful in obtaining their (business) goals.

7. Invite your Next Gen to accept uncertainty as a resource:

Because life and in particular business life is unpredictable, there is always uncertainty involved. The worst that can happen when one is confronted by uncertainty is to freeze and take no action whatsoever. Teach your Next Gen by example that uncertainty actually is a resource that can help you take better and more balanced decisions.

Uncertainty is closely connected to risk and you want to teach risk awareness but not risk phobia to your future leaders.

How to do this? Create an atmosphere that shows you encourage Next Gen's initiatives. Avoid a culture of reckoning. Allow them to take decisions under uncertainty and help them be prepared to take risks. Show them how to face the uncertain risky situation at hand, to consider all possible options, to choose what seems wisest, then watch the results and act accordingly. Discuss the consequences, positive or negative, in a constructive manner and always ask them: "what have you learned from this?"

8. Turn conflicts into resources:

Living in harmony – obviously – is easier, nicer, and probably more productive. But people all too often regard conflict as something that absolutely and by all means must be avoided. A black-white stance where harmony is perfect and conflict is evil, disregards human nature in which emotions, differences of opinions, and conflicting interests are mundane. A conflict-phobia can lead to fossilization that does not allow different points of view and therefore can block growth. The solution-focused thinking sees conflicts as an unavoidable and natural phenomenon. Even more so, conflicts can be seen as resources: from the clash of ideas, progress emerges.

The essence of the solution-focused approach is searching for what is common between conflicting parties. This communality forms the basis for communication and negotiation between conflicting parties that ideally ends in a compromise. A compromise is defined as an outcome that is acceptable to all parties without necessarily making every separate party totally happy.

9. Excellence tops perfection:

Ambitious young people with successful parents tend to strive for replicating the parent's achievements. That in itself is great. In this quest they can – alas – stumble into the fallacy of perfection where good is never good enough. When everything always must be the absolute best, when the reaching of the moon is the baseline for their (lust for) achievements, failure unavoidably sits waiting patiently around the corner.

If your Next Gen shows signs of obsessive perfectionism, you can both be both happy ("they are motivated, ambitious, full of energy and lust for life") and anxious ("they are on a straight course to failure, burnout and debilitating disappointment"). This is a stage direction that they need your guidance to steer them away from the booby-trap of perfectionism.

The following ideas can be helpful when you gently offer your Next Gen some guidance.

"You can never know what is good, let alone what is perfect. But you can always know what is better. Stick with better." -Steve de Shazer

"Striving for perfection helps you stretch yourself towards greater accomplishments. But beware of muscle ruptures." -Kristos Olympiakis

"Perfection is not attainable but if we chase perfection, we can catch excellence." -Vince Lombardi

"By being excellent, you buy your freedom." -Mathieu Weggeman

10. Show your Next Gen that Work, like Life, is JOYOUS.

Let's not be naive, life and by extension business life is not always a walk in the park. Life can be tedious, boring, frightening, confusing, etc. Yet, Life is a miracle in itself that deserves to be celebrated.

The same goes for your life in business. Approaching problems as challenges and finding solutions to your challenges can be exhilarating. The result of hard and smart work is rewarding. This gives you joy.

Celebrate and share your joy with everyone around you and especially with your offspring. How? Tell them, show them, whistle a tune, dance, raise the glass even if it's with champagne or chocolate milk, it doesn't matter and toast – literally or metaphorically – with your children.

Chapter 5

The Big Question

Somewhere in Phase 3 of the family@business life cycle, the Next Gen comes to an age at which they start to make long-term career decisions. Decisions taken at this stage are crucial for the future. Now comes a delicate time: will one or more of your children step into the family@business? If not, you have to consider alternative scenarios that we will explain in Chapter 12. If yes, then the following Big Question needs to be considered carefully before they can step into the Next Generation leadership and become entrepreneurs.

The Big Question

The Big Question is simple: does the Next Gen have what it takes to lead the family@business toward the future? The answer is complex.

When you break down this Big Question into its constituent parts, this question even can become downright complicated:

1   Do they want to do it?
2   Do they have what it takes?
3   Are they able to do it?
4   Do they love to do it?
5   Will there be a "primus under pares" or will they do it together?

To answer question 1, all you have to do is ask it. But, is it that simple? No, it is not. First of all, there is the question of timing. When do you ask this question? Of course, not when the children are ten years old. On the other hand, some founder-owners refuse to ask the children this fundamental question because they are convinced for some mysterious reason that the children should take the initiative as some kind of proof that they are interested. This can lead to a strange situation where both parties are waiting for each other: the parents think that the children are not interested, while the children think that the parents are not willing to give them a chance. The mutual frustration that can result from this is counterproductive. So, don't!

DOI: 10.4324/9781003194200-5

So then, when do you ask this question? When the time is right. And that is different for every person and for every family. Since the family@business, as you have seen in Chapter 1, often is the "eldest child," lots of – even kitchen table – conversations are about the business. So, the children are involved in a natural way and the time to discuss this question will come naturally. Some families discuss this question in a more formal manner, e.g. when the time has come for the children to choose what they will study. Whatever fits best with your family, works best for you.

There are two things to watch out for. First, make it crystal clear to your children that this question is purely informative. Make sure you don't ask the question in such a way that the children are implicitly forced to answer yes. Second, allow and accept that the answer may vary over time. Saying "no" today can become a "yes" over time, and vice versa.

In this chapter, you will find useful tools that will help you to answer questions 2 and 3. The ten Leadership Potential Indicators can not only be used to assess where everyone stands but can also be used as a continuous exercise to further refine your necessary skills.

Chapter 12 answers question 4 and provides you with elements to help you make one of the most important decisions of your life: Shall I dedicate my life to the family@business? If working in the family@business is only a second choice because you like to do other things, think twice. However, if you feel that the family@business is the love of your life, go for it.

Chapter 6 is about the challenge of working with your siblings. Chapter 10 shows how this works in practice and Chapter 11 gives you tools to answer question 5.

John and Annie

Sitting on the dock of the bay at their weekend house, John and Annie like to reminisce. In their early fifties now, they like to talk about how it all went with the business and the family. By now, Eric is 28 and working as the vice-president of R&D. Ella is in her fifth year in medical school. Cherly was not very successful in her studies and works as a non-executive in the marketing department of the Family@business.

Looking back is for fun times while looking at the future is what the entrepreneurial couple does for a living.

Annie: John, what is your biggest wish for the future?
John: well, I do hope that the company will be continued and that further growth goes together with stable results. Not only our family is depending on this but also the families of all our employees. What about you, Annie?
Annie: I am a little bit afraid that it will be complicated to find a way that all three of our kids will be treated fair and equal. I know we all love

> *them equally, but we can not be blind for the fact they are so different. They have very different capabilities.*

John: *I keep thinking of that proverb by, who was it again, Thomas Jefferson or Plato, I don't remember: "Nothing is more unequal than the equal treatment of unequal people."*

Annie: *It was that famous Dutch geneticist, Galjaard who said this.*

John: *Your memory still is acute, my dear Annie.*

Annie: *Thanks. Clearly Ella will not come to work for the family@business. She is pursuing her lifelong dream.*

John: *Yeah, and Cherly still is struggling to find her path in the company. Her gig in marketing, to be frank and honest is not the biggest of success, according to her manager.*

Annie: *Eric is on his way up. But doing a good job still is different from taking the whole of the company on his shoulders. I don't know if he has it in him to step in your shoes, John.*

John: *Well, he is still young. We have to allow him some more years of training and growing as a manager. By the way, never forget that someone will have to step into our shoes, Annie, because you were and remain at least as important as me over all those years. Now the question of treating the children equally in the financial sense doesn't worry me. We will find a way there. This is just a matter of distributing our wealth in equal parts and we have many financial specialists that can help us in this field. What worries me more is if Eric can do it, take the leadership position.*

Annie: *What I worry about is how they will interact in the future, when they no longer are just siblings but also co-owners of the company.*

Assessment

Classically this problem is tackled by a competency assessment that gives a lot of useful information. Yet future success can't be predicted from past performance. Even banks know this when they offer you an investment opportunity. Plus, a competency assessment is a static picture that can never predict future developments.

Work in Progress

Leadership depends not only on the personality but also on the circumstances in which leadership needs to be developed, honed, fine-tuned, and used. Leadership needs to be deserved in the heart and minds of the people who choose to follow you. Leadership is never a given nor fixed (unless you are a dictator) but always a mandate in continuous flux. Leadership is a Work-in-Progress.

Basic Tools

The fact that there is no fail-proof template for perfect leadership lies at the heart of the uncertainty around the answer to the Big Question. What however is common to all successful (future) Family@business leaders is a continuous learning-to-learn stance combined with the soft skills for working with people and their needs.

Trait or Skill

The basic tools are powered by the presence of traits and skills that are indicators for the potentiality of your leadership. One can argue that these indicators are inborn traits that one person has more than another. One can also easily argue that these indicators are skills that can be acquired and honed. This is the old discussion about Nurture versus Nature. We prefer to see it as Nature AND Nurture, traits AND skills.

John and Annie

John: We have to talk to the three of them. Doesn't matter if we already know Ella's decision for her career. She still will be a shareholder, just like the others.

Annie: Well, we think we know her decision but, you are right, better ask her in the open. The same goes for Cherly. It doesn't look like she plans to go for an executive function, but we have to keep her options open. Besides, we never had this kind of conversation with our children. It was not necessary up until now. We better prepare for our future, which is also their future. Not to forget the future of the company.

John: Mind you, I do not even think about stepping down from my big chair (both laugh). But maybe the time has come to step aside little by little.

John and Annie decided that they would talk to their kids separately. The children were happy that moment finally had come. Ella repeated her decision firmly. John jokingly suggested that she better become a gerontologist so that she could take care of her parents in old age. Cherly was in tears, telling that she felt that she isn't up to the task of taking care of the business. Her parents consoled her and told her that it is a great resource if a person has the courage to face her capabilities. 'No use reaching for the moon when you don't feel this is in your possibilities. But, dear Cherly, you are still very young, you have time to find your path in life and work. Try your best and you will find your path'.

Eric, by now successful in his executive position, admitted that sometimes he also had doubts about himself: *"Mom and Dad, I like my job, I think I am reasonably successful in it. Yet I know that I still have to learn so much from you."*

Annie: *We are not leaving the company, Eric, well, not yet. Would it help you if we found a method that can help you become more confident?*
Eric: *That would be great!*
John: *Lately I was at a seminar where some professor talked about leadership indicators. She also developed a tool to facilitate growth. You want me to give professor Cynthia Hange a call?*

Ten Indicators of Leadership Potential

1   Love for learning
    One can also call this "curiosity": always seeking novel information, experiences, and knowledge. Curiosity fuels investigating things that lie beyond one's own line of work and initial interest. New and novel information thus obtained, facilitates change and creates a learning mindset.

    To paraphrase Heather McGowan: "In a world that is as volatile as ours, where complexity is the norm, where the only certainty is uncertainty, where the acceleration of change keeps accelerating, *learning becomes more important than knowing."*

2   Love for feedback
    Constantly seeking candid feedback on whatever you are contributing, ameliorates your fit with your environment (be it people or ideas) and facilitates positive working relations. This feedback loop is one big learning accelerator for creating and accruing knowledge that in itself invites continuous learning. Being open to and even asking for feedback means that you are not afraid to show your vulnerability in a business environment where this is sometimes seen as a weakness.

3   Creativity
    Creativity is the ability to gather and rearrange information in such a way that new and previously unseen possibilities emerge. Creative leadership is the ability to unleash creativity in others. Or: use the same information that is available for everybody and create new insights by thinking out of the box.

4   Effective communication
    What good is learning and new knowledge if you do not have an accurate way of sharing it with others? Because information grows by sharing, your network and therefore you become more intelligent. Effective communicators have the skill to offer their information in such a manner that the other wants to receive and use it.

5 Emotional Intelligence (EQ)

From the science of swarm intelligence, we know that intelligence resides not only in the individual but – even more – so in the interrelations between individuals. Networks are more intelligent than the sum of all individual intelligent agents in that network. Entrepreneurship is in essence working with humans within their network of humans (combined with non-biologically silicon-based intelligence, computers, and software). In this area EQ trumps IQ. That is why you need EQ on top of your IQ, otherwise you would never be in the position of successor.

The leading exponent on this topic, Daniel Goleman,[1] tells us: "Generally, IQ determines what job you can get and hold, while EQ predicts how well you will do in that career – whether you have the motivation and social abilities to be a star performer or leader."

"Emotional Intelligence" is defined by Daniel Goleman as the "The capacity for recognizing our own feelings, for motivating ourselves, and for managing emotions well in ourselves." Simply put: Self-awareness and self-management.

6 Social Intelligence[2]

On the flip side of the intelligence coin, we find social intelligence (SI). SI is defined as: "The capacity for sensing what others are feeling, the skill to manage relationships in diverse situations including conflict resolution, and the ability to influence others."

Simply put empathy and interactional skills.

7 Determination, Persistence, and Resilience

Showing determination and resilience when faced with – unavoidable – difficulties, adversity and plain bad luck in (business) life predicts the degree of success that you will have as a leader. There is a direct correlation between your degree of determination to bring things to the best possible end and success in life. Mind you: determination does not equal stubbornness.

8 Long-term vision

Archetypal for family businesses is that they think of the long term and therefore it is crucial that their leaders have the capacity and the passion for strategic thinking. Managing your family@business for the long haul is only possible through a combination of daily excellence and proactive adapting to future possibilities. We can't shape the macro-economic vicissitudes, but we can surf on those ever-changing waves while keeping a keen eye on the long-term direction that we want to move toward.

9 Pragmatic Realism

Naiveté, seeing the world through pink glasses, believing that if you do your utter best to think as positively as possible is as effective as thinking a rabbit's paw will save your life in a war. Insisting that a half-full bottle is the only reality and that there is no such thing as a half-empty bottle, denies the fact that a half-empty bottle contains exactly the same reality as a half-full bottle. Pragmatic realism teaches you to face the reality in the bottle while defining it as half full. Such pragmatic realism helps you to survive in the desert. Pragmatic realism values common sense above complicated book wisdom.

10   Optimism

Business by definition is risky business. Without the belief that something good comes out of it, without hope, nobody would swap certainty for possible failure. Calculated risks still are risks so you need optimism, the mental attitude that whatever happens, one can always strive for the best possible results. Karl Popper, the famous social philosopher taught us: Optimism is a Moral Duty.

> *Hope is to the human mind what oxygen is to our lungs.*
> *Froma Walsh*

Dynamic Assessment

Both G1 and the Next Gen can use the indicators to assess at every moment where they stand. G1 can reflect where on a scale from 0 (nothing at all) to 10 (perfect), his successors are. The Next Generation can use this tool to self-assess where they are on the same scales.

This dynamic assessment shows where your resources are and what you can do to improve them. You will discover which aspects of your personal style you can hone to become more effective. Discovering that you have rather low scores on some indicators, will help you compensate by putting more accent on the indicators that you are strong in. This will give you time to slowly research for yourself if and how you can ameliorate the other indicators.

Since it is a dynamic assessment, it will help you surf the waves of change in both your personal life and in your business life to the best of your abilities.

Everybody has to realize that this tool is what it is: a tool. It is not a precise measurement instrument of leadership potential. In a complex, ever-changing world where the business environment is uncertain, volatile, and ambiguous. Pretending that a mathematically precise leadership tool exists is pretentious, stupid, and even dangerous.

Open communication about the results of this dynamic assessment offers a powerful answer to the Big Question.

Box   Boost your Leadership Potential: the BLEEP Exercise

In order to train yourself and further hone the skillful use of the ten indicators, you might do this exercise on a yearly basis.

1   Consider each indicator and give yourself a number on a scale where 0 stands for: "not applicable to me at all" and ten stands for: "totally applicable to me."
2   Think about what it is that you already do so that you can give yourself that number (and write down your answers). Make this as concrete as possible for yourself.
3   Ask yourself: what is the smallest step that I could take to make progress on this element? What do I need to do differently to get to a higher number? Write down in as much detail and with as much concrete examples as you can think of.
4   How will my co-workers notice this little progress?
5   Create a plan in which you translate all that you have discovered about yourself into a concrete improvement strategy.
6   Repeat this exercise every six months and joyfully add these incremental improvements to your leadership style.

If you have enough self-confidence, ask people you trust to do this same exercise with you in mind. Then have an open discussion with them.

G1 can do the same exercise and compare their insights with the findings of the Next Gen. Difficult? Yes. Unusual? Sure. Powerful? Certainly!

John and Annie

Annie: *I am so glad we invited Professor Cynthia Hange. She gave a wonderful workshop on those ten indicators, explaining exactly how to use them in order to get maximum information and at the same time preventing a static view on leadership.*

John: *Yeah, she was great, Pity that only Eric and Ella wanted to take the first Boost Your Leadership Potential Exercise. What a name! Let's call it the BLPE, or even better: BLEEP...*

Annie: *Cherly probably was afraid of the outcome so she skipped the opportunity. It was no use explaining to her that this exercise is not*

an exam but just a tool to help one become better. What a pity. Well,
maybe later

John: *Anyhow, the other kids liked it. And they recognized themselves in the*
challenges that lie ahead for their career. I wonder if they will follow
up on their decision to do this BLEEP every year.

Annie: *I also hope that they will follow Prof. C.Hange's suggestion to discuss*
the results with us, with each other and with the people they
work with.

John: *That will be the case for Eric. I don't know if it fits for Ella working*
in the hospital. But she can do it for herself and we will help her.
Doctors also have to be leaders in their work. By the way, maybe it is
a good idea to ask our management team to do the BLEEP for
themselves. Well, we will see about the timing of that. Whatever the
BLEEP, the most important thing is that we have started talking
openly about these issues and that was about time. I should have done
that far earlier.

Annie: *Water under the bridge, dear John. Today is today and we made a*
significant step towards the future of our family and the family@
business.

Conclusion

Answering the Big Question (who of the children is able and willing to rise
to the challenge of succeeding G1?) is *the* essential step that enables both
Founders and Successors to take the giant step toward the future of the
family@business. When these Big Questions are not addressed in the correct
manner, the Family@business' future is built on a quagmire.

Of course, answering the Big Question is just one step. Later we will have
to address the question of ownership, shareholder-ship, dealing with stakeholders, wealth management, etc.

But for now: so far, so good. Let us move on and see what challenges the
Next Generation faces.

Notes

1 Interview with Daniel Goleman, reference: http://www.abhijitbhaduri.com/index.php/
2010/12/emotional-intelligence-matters-more-than-iq/
2 http://www.mysocialintelligence.com/the-relationship-between-social-intelligence-
and-emotional-intelligence/

Chapter 6

Challenges for the Next Generation

Now your time as G2 is coming. How to proceed? What are the important issues that you, the upcoming generation need to understand in order to both respect the work of your parents and create space for your young energy?

After discovering how strong you are in each of the ten leadership indicators as you discovered in the BLEEP exercise, you can design a way to permanently hone your skills. When you feel confident that you have what it takes, the time has come for you to step in as the next generation.

As we learned in the Five Phase Model (Chapter 2), by the time you are between 25 and 35 years old, the family@business has become large and complex. You have finished your studies, maybe even added some extra certifications, got yourself an MBA, and are probably in the process of creating your own family. You have taken the first steps into the family@ business and you did so with success. You are now in middle management and very busy with an operational and/or executive job.

Confronted with the extra weight that rests upon your shoulders as a family member, you have much more on your plate than just your daily job. People, both inside the company as well as from the outside are watching you.

As a successor, you are confronted with many problems, some simple, some complicated, and some downright complex. Some of the more poignant problems are: how to morph from child (they have seen me in short pants!!) into leader, how to show respect for my parents when I want things to change, how will I gain the trust of all the stakeholders who have known no one else but my parents as business owners, and last but not least, how will I deal with my siblings. Big problems!

John and Annie

On the flight back home after a visit to one of their foreign subsidiaries, John and Annie share all of the information that they gathered during that visit. By now their family@business has grown into a complex organization. They have

DOI: 10.4324/9781003194200-6

key persons on all the important functions in the company. Some of them have been working in the company for a long time.

Annie: I am afraid that it will be very hard for the kids.

John: What do you mean?

Annie: When you, well we, founded the company we had nothing to lose. The only thing that could happen was that we failed early on. Then we just could have started all over and done something else.

John: True, but why are you afraid for the kids?

Annie: Well, think about all the problems that they will have to face. Together we will have to find a way to make room for them to find their own place in life. I know for a fact that they love us and that they do not want to hurt us. But they have to find their own way in life.

John: We can't protect them against the vicissitudes of life.

Annie: That is not what I mean, John. I have total faith in the fact that all of our three children, however different they are, have all that it takes to find their path in life. What worries me more is that we inevitably will have clashes, especially with Eric when he moves up in the business.

John: Isn't that a bit pessimistic, Annie?

Annie: No, John, that is realism. If all goes well, Eric will have to compete with you and you are not the easiest person to deal with when it comes to joint business decisions, let alone sharing your power.

John: I hate to say it but you are right. So, as in so many things in our life, I again need your help in this. What worries me more is that Eric and the other kids will avoid competing with me because they respect me too much. I will do my utter best to make sure that I give Eric enough leeway to settle his own course. And when you notice that I put my foot down too hard on him, please hit me over the head when we are alone.

   (Both laugh)

Annie: They will be scrutinized by our personnel as well as by the outsiders because they all will become shareholders and will have big influence on how the business will be run in the future.

John: Eric is well liked, and he has already proved to be very good in his job, hard working too. And Ella, well, apart from always being present at every company party, she is not in the company. Cherly might be a little bit of a problem. For now, she has no ambition further than her today's job, but she is still young.

Annie: *Today all is peace and harmony among our kids but with the succession things might change. There is a lot of money and power involved and we have to help them prepare for this. See, John, why I am a little bit afraid for the future. There are so many problems coming over the horizon.*

Formula P

If you choose to make your life lighter, you can reframe every problem as a wish for change that, with the right approach, can be translated into a challenge.

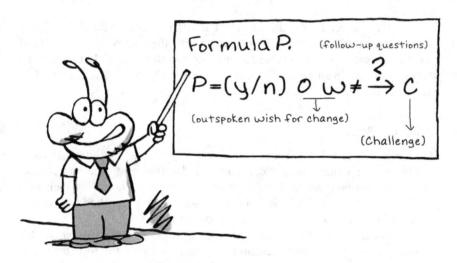

How to do this? Simple but not easy! Take a problem in your mind and ask yourself: what do I want instead? Then ask yourself: what do I need to make the smallest step toward the "instead." Now your wish for change magically has turned into a challenge.

This approach helps us to embrace problems for the simple reason: the more problems, the more wishes for change, the more "in stead's" and thus the more challenges.

Four Challenges for the Next Gen

Given Formula P, when successors face problems in succession, they now know that solution-focused thinking and working can translate those problems into challenges.

Challenge 1 Morphing from Child/Offspring to Employee to Leader

The successor may have been working as an employee in the Family Business for some time before the first steps in the succession process take place. During this phase, one is a son/daughter and employee: two roles that are much easier to combine than son/daughter and manager with executive responsibilities. When the Next Generation moves up toward a managerial position, the chances are much greater that she will enter the sphere of influence that her parent occupies in the company. This overlapping phase always happens, with the exception of the sudden death of the parent. Then comes the time the child-employee moves into a top management and/or board position and takes up a corporate leadership role.

With each career move, the successor needs to morph into another role and assume another position. With each move, the successor and G1 need to learn to slowly but decisively separate family and business. In the end, the successor is the business leader during the workweek and is the child in the weekend's family gatherings.

Challenge 2 Respect

It is evident that G1 was successful in his/her business or otherwise there was no business that needs succession. G1 deserves gratitude and respect for their accomplishments. Next Gen shows respect by honoring their predecessors' work just like it is good to honor their parenthood. Showing respect however is something else than idolatry.

At the same time, G2 needs self-respect and self-trust to step in the footsteps of the previous generation. But stepping into the footsteps does not mean replicating. The only constant in both business and Life is change, so there is no alternative for the Next Gen but to change things.

The classic scheme is that in the beginning when G2 enters the family@ business, G2 shows respect for G1 by adopting their way of doing things. Confronted with the need for change, G2 then adapts their own way of thinking and working. Finally, G2 changes their methods to accommodate the necessity of evolution in business life. In this process, the Next Gen gradually must find its own voice. Changing from successor to transferee (e.g. the difference between being handed the company versus taking it over) gives the transferring generation the confidence that the Next Gen takes things in hand. In this delicate balancing act of giving and taking responsibility, both business and family relationships (will) come under pressure from time to time. To make this transition successful, the successor requires a well-balanced cocktail of competencies (CH 5 Leadership indicators) and skills (which you will learn in the next chapter).

Challenge 3 Trust

The main assets of all companies in the world are its workers, from the most low-level jobs to the highest positions in the corporate hierarchy. The main currency that facilitates cooperation is trust.

As Next Gen, besides learning the intricacies of your business, it is an absolute necessity that you gain the trust of the employees, from the operational level in the factory to the highest-ranked non-family manager. Moreover, you can rest assured that stakeholders outside your family@business, from your banker to your customers, keep a close eye on "the family newcomer." They all see you as the future and everybody wants to see what the future looks like...

The Beatles taught us: "Money can't buy you love." The same goes for trust: trust can't be bought it can only be earned. So as Next Gen, there is no way around the fact that you will have to work hard to gain this trust. Plus, you will have to keep working at it for a long, long time. And the results of your hard work, certainly in the beginning, are fragile because trust grows slowly but evaporates fast.

Like it or not, you will be scrutinized and tested. And there is no way to avoid or circumvent this: it comes with your name. So be prepared for this, work hard and show in action that you do not occupy your position because you have the same surname as your parents-owners.

> Trust and hope are the only legal performance-enhancing drugs.
> Dov Seidman (in Friedman, T. 2016)

Challenge 4 Siblings

As an only child, you will have no trouble with your siblings but the price for this is that you are alone in your generation. Being an only child and heir can put a lot of weight on your shoulders, especially when you do not feel like taking over the business. Yet when you have lust for business, being an only child is the simplest constellation in the succession scenario.

When you have siblings, it becomes more challenging. You will have to work toward a well-balanced working relationship with all of them. Even if not everybody will participate in the succession and come to work in the family@business, they all are inheritors and will become co-owners over time.

It becomes complex when your family@business consists of two branches in the family. Then you have nieces and nephews involved in the company.

Here the Next Gen will have to build a "Nephieces" team, like Prof. Jozef Lievens, a Belgian family@business expert, calls those teams.

When your company comes into G3 or more, the family constellation can become complicated. This situation needs special care because by that time, the company is running on itself and there is more need to manage the family. This can be done in many ways: culling the family tree, separating ownership from corporate management, using holding structures, etc. One of the most important tools one can use is the Family Charter, a document that states all the values, expectations, and rules of conduct within the family@business. This is such a helpful tool that we will go into detail in Chapter 16 where you will find examples and tools.

Whatever method one chooses, respect and trust always are the basic ingredients for success.

> Collaboration moves at the speed of trust.
>> Chris Thompson (in Friedman, T. 2016)

Whatever is your special case, The challenge is managing the family relationships in such a way that the involved family members form a T.E.A.M: Together Each Achieves More.

John and Annie

Annie: What a good idea to translate these problems into challenges. Without this insight, we might ponder away for ages about all the problems, where they come from and to what possible disasters they might lead.

John: Correct. Now, with that Formula P, we all are looking forwards into a hopeful future. Tackling challenges is precisely what we as an entrepreneurial family are good at.

Annie: Our children all are very respectful and trustworthy, both towards the family as towards the company. However they will behave amongst themselves, we can only stand by and support them.

John: As parents and employers we can help them to gradually take steps towards adulthood so that they find their own way of positioning themselves both in their personal life as well as in our organization.

Annie: Besides the challenges for the children, let us not forget that we as Founders also have some challenges ahead of us. Since we founded the company, we have known no other life than a life for *family and company. The children are finding their own way and we just have to make sure that – however well-meant – we are not in their way. We have to prepare for our succession.*

John: *I am well aware this is more than finding good legal, financial and fiscal methods. That expertise can be bought. The technical experts can show us all the possibilities but we still have to do the thinking about what it is that we want for the future.*

Annie: *Both the children and ourselves have a lot of homework in front of us.*

John: *This homework has to be done while the daily hustling and bustling of the business continues. As they say, the show must go on!*

Now the Stage Is Set

If you are the transferring party G1, go to the next Chapter 7.

If you are the Next Gen, the transferee, you might choose to go to Chapter 11.

How to Prepare GI for Succession

Late in Phase 3 and certainly in Phase 4 (see Chapter 2), the Founding Generation must start the process of thinking, talking, and acting upon their – inevitable – succession. Both the ownership succession and the management succession are crucial for the survival of the family@business.

John and Annie

John, a businessman of 57 years old, is sitting in his home office on a Saturday morning. Tired after a week of travel, negotiations, big decisions, and in general lots of hard work and stress, he tries to relax. His thoughts go to all that happened in the last 30 years: how he got married and right afterward started his construction software business on a very small scale, the difficulties in the first years of the fragile company, his first big contracts but also the moments of darkness where failure seemed imminent. So many life or death situations: negotiations for one particularly big transaction kept dragging on and the cash drain on the fragile company was life-threatening, his first big client went broke and he was not sure if the insurance would cover all costs. He remembers the anxieties, the worries, the sleepless nights. John decides to stop this negative line of thinking. But he also remembers the proudness he shared with his young wife whenever they made a small step forward with the company.

With a tea in hand, John thinks about the future. He is proud of their children: a son of 32, a daughter of 27 who is on her way of becoming a medical specialist, and a daughter of 24 who works in the company, albeit in non-executive position. They are grown up and yet they are still so young. As happens very often in the last months, John starts musing about the future and he is concerned. What will happen with his life work, the company? The Big Question "are they capable of taking over?" has been answered positively for Eric, the son who is on his way up in the organization. Ella, the second daughter has made it clear that she will definitely not work in the family@business since she is totally focused on her career in medicine. Cherly, the youngest, shows no other interest than her 9-to-5 job

DOI: 10.4324/9781003194200-7

in the marketing department. She is more interested in fashion, shopping and having a good time with her friends.

Preparing for Succession

When most Family Business owners think of succession, what first comes to mind are issues like: what are the financial, fiscal, and inheritance rights consequences? How will the kids be able to pay for all of this? Almost always, these technical issues are the first to be discussed with the company lawyer, the accountant, and maybe with some friends-entrepreneurs. Are these technical issues important? Sure. Are they the most important? Absolutely not! Solutions to these technical issues can be purchased from the respective experts. Research shows that once the emotional minefield is cleared, the solution to these technical issues is almost self-evident. But if one makes the mistake of focusing exclusively on these technical matters, there will be a price to pay later on in the succession process: disconnection within the family or between family and non-family management, psychological issues that have not been outspoken and therefore remain unsolved, technical solutions that camouflage the fact that the Founders in reality do now wish to step back, ...

Much more important and much more difficult to tackle, let alone answer, are the emotional, psychological, and relational issues. These issues are connected to the given that all individuals, families, and family businesses, go through a cycle of development. To say that the eternal wheel of existence, in other words the succession of generations within the family and the company, poses challenges is evident. On top of this, since first-generation entrepreneurs have no experience with succession, it all is a novelty, a scaring novelty.

John and Annie Invite a Family@business Consultant

What is John to do in the face of this complex, difficult and challenging situation? Doing nothing is not an option since life goes on and John simply knows that he can't escape reality.

John soon realizes that if he wants his company and family to prepare for the future, he first needs to work on himself. That was true when he started his company: what do I want to be and become?

Like always he shares his thoughts with Annie who admits that she hasn't got a clue of where to start. Together they decide to find a family@business specialist. They consult with their external accountant and with the family lawyer. They both offer the same name: Mark.

John and Annie decide to embark on a personal journey into themselves and decide to talk with a family@business consultant who has a track record in this field.

Already in their first meeting, Mark offers recognition and appreciation, not only for their business and family success but most of all for the fact that they have the courage to think of the future of their life's work.

Mark:	*OK, now that you have told me the story of your life and how you came about to start your business, let's move on, shall we?*
Annie:	*I must say it feels really good to be able to tell our story to an outsider. It brings so many memories that I haven't thought about in ages.*
John:	*We told you only the great stories. The ugly ones are for later. (laughing)*
Mark:	*We will come to those later; at least if you think they are relevant for the future.*
John:	*Can you tell us a bit how you work? What are we supposed to do? Do you have a format for this kind of process? Remember I am an engineer.*
Mark:	*I will share with you the steps I usually take. These have proven to be successful in many cases. But every case, every family and Family@business is different. I will tailor it to what is most useful to your situation. Besides, strict stepwise procedures, however useful and even necessary in more mechanical situations, tend not to fit the complexity of each family@business case. And I certainly do not want to create a Bed of Procrustes.*
Annie:	*A bed of what…?*
Mark:	*Procrustes was an innkeeper in Ancient Greece. In his free time, he liked to do woodworks. Procrustes crafted a beautiful bed. Guests that stayed too late or had too much to drink, were allowed to stay over and sleep in this bed, for free. There was only one condition: the bed was 1.70 cm long and the guest needed to fit exactly in the bed. If the guest was 1.67 cm, he was stretched until he was 1.70 cm. If he was 1.75 cm tall, the guest could choose from which side 5 cm was to be cut.*
John and Annie are laughing:	*Crazy story.*
Mark:	*All too often and with the best of intentions, coaching and consultancy models are crafted like a bed of Procrustes. An elegant 10 step model is devised and then cast into a protocol. All that remains is to find a family@business client that fits exactly into this model.*
John:	*Great business model but I am glad that you will not use it upon us. We just want the best and the best is what fits*

precisely with the needs and possibilities of our family and our company.

Mark: *And that is exactly what we are going to do. First, I will ask you to do some homework around more philosophical and existential themes.*

Annie: *Remember we are simple businesspeople so don't make it too complicated please.*

John: *And do not beat around the bush.*

Mark: *It is pretty straightforward what I will ask you but still I want you to take some time to prepare yourselves. This is the kind of big questions where the answer is less important than the search for an answer.*

John and Annie: *OK*

Mark: *We will then discuss these items and my task is to ask you questions. Your task is to do your best and be open towards yourself. If ever we come across topics that you do not want to talk about, just tell me. After the two of you feel comfortable with your findings, we will talk with the children. You can choose to have that conversation amongst you as a family or maybe you feel more comfortable if I participate as facilitator. We will decide when we get to that point.*

Annie: *Let's go.*

Mark: *You don't have to remember the following questions. I have put them on paper for you. Let me go over them and. Please, feel invited to ask questions and add topics or issues that you deem important. Best is to take some time to think and write down some ideas, thoughts and feelings. These notes will form the base for our next conversations. You might do this alone or together, whatever you see as the most useful. I prefer that you answer them first on your own and afterwards have a conversation between the two of you before we meet next time. But you decide. Here we go:*

- *What are my goals for the next part of my life, both personally and in business?*
- *How will I cope with the fact that after my succession, the person John/Annie will no longer coincide with the entrepreneur John/Annie?*
- *How will my family, my friends, social network and business relations change when I will be no longer "the" company person?*
- *What will I do in order not to become bored?*
- *How will I find meaning in my life after a life of only work?*

Annie:	*These are rather philosophical questions.*
Mark:	*Correct. And like I told you, the answers are less important than searching for the answers.*
John:	*Remarkable. Your questions prime us to envision a future beyond our company.*
Annie:	*This is going to be tough because we hardly ever, well, actually we never, thought about a life without the company.*
Mark:	*Sure, that is normal for Founders- Owners that created a business. The company is your eldest child, remember?*
John:	*Well, there is no way around this succession stuff unless we could have eternal life. (All laugh)*

Ten Best Practices for Preparing GI toward Succession

1 Accept that you are lonely when going through these existential questions: you can only answer for yourself.

   Being an entrepreneur means that you are constantly in contact with others and the outside world. Your focus is mostly instrumental for what you want to accomplish. You test your decisions with others who are close to you in the work.

   When you confront yourself with the future of your post-entrepreneur life, you realize that you are on your own. Nobody, not even the person closest to you in life, can answer these existential questions for you.

2 Find a – preferably neutral – interlocutor with whom you can find trust to have open conversations.

   Just like you can't see the colors of your eyes without a mirror or someone telling you, it is easier to reflect on these existential questions with another person as a sounding board. The more neutral this sounding board is, the more you will be able to hear your own voice.

3 Offer yourself ample time to slowly but carefully go through all the existential questions without rushing yourself.

   This work is no rational business plan that needs swift decisions. This work is a lifetime process that deserves germinating time. After a lifetime of finding meaningfulness in work, now the time has come to find meaningfulness in other aspects of life. And you will notice that, once you start this work, it is a never-ending story of discovery.

4 Accept that there are no right or wrong answers but only mind- and heart-opening questions that demand emotional courage.

   These existential questions are not a quiz where the answers are right or wrong. Most family@business people have spent most of their time and career (which for Founder-Owners is about the same) thinking, planning, and worrying about the business. There was not much time for thinking about their personal lives. Today, the succession is an inescapable next step if they want their eldest child, the company, to survive. If they want a full life for their remaining days on earth, they have to take the courage to open-mindedly face their personal answers to these questions. Some answers will be joyful and happy. Some answers will be confrontational and maybe even painful. But, hey, that is life!

5   Invest time in your life partner and family so that you prepare for a family life in which the company slowly recedes into the background.

Founders – Owners have spent most of their time and energy to make the family@business a thriving business. Their lives have evolved with and revolve around the family@business. However discouraging and stressful all those years of building, growing, and maintaining the family@business may have been, it was also fun, exciting, and adventurous. Now you are entering the next phase of your life, as a person, as a family, and as an entrepreneur and this implies that you better let your attention slowly evolve from family@business to family life. The children have shifted to their own lives and the founder-owner couple must find new ways to be together without the company's binding factor.

6   In order to be able to let go, you need to get hold of other things, preferably activities that will give you a new meaning in life.

This can be anything. From golf, tennis, or other sports over classic cars, art, travel, music till voluntary service for charitable causes. Some of the bigger families enter the field of philanthropy. What you choose is of minor importance. That you choose with your heart is essential. And it works best if you share at least some of your alternative activities with your partner. Oh, and of course, if you are lucky, there are always the grandchildren.

7   Create room for open conversations with the children about all possible scenarios for the future and start this by asking them how they see their own future, in and out of the company.

It is best that you as "mater and pater familias" initiate the conversations with your children. The reason for this is simple: from a certain age of the children, they know, together with all other stakeholders of the family@business, that succession is on the way. Not talking about this is ignoring the elephant in the room.

Some families are not used to having these kinds of conversations. Some families may need some help from a professional outsider such as a psychologist, coach, or a reliable advisor who has connections with the family and the family@business but is able to stay in a neutral position. For other families, this is rather natural. Anyway, if you want to avoid problems in the future, there's no other way.

8　Experiment with taking a day off during the week so that you get used to working less and delegating more.

Most founders of a family@business simply do not know what a nine-to-five job is. They have worked long hours, on weekends and during holidays. Their calendars were filled by the needs of the company. So, working less is probably working hard, especially working less without feeling guilty. But you already have the resources to do that. When you founded a family@business, you soon realized that you can't do this on your own. You hired competent people and let them do their job. You've only supervised. Sure, in the beginning you checked them and even took the work out of their hands because you were convinced that it was better, faster, and cheaper to do it yourself. Soon you collapsed into the wall of overstrain and began to delegate. Now it's time to strengthen your delegating behavior. How to do this? Use the "Plan-Do-Trust" formula and judge on the basis of the results, or even better, have someone else check the results and report this information to you.

9　The emotional hard work on your succession inevitably confronts you with the fact of your mortality.

One of the main reasons why the topic of succession in family@ business is (too often) postponed is the fact that people do not like to be confronted with their end. You often hear arguments for this postponement such as: "There is still plenty of time. We consider ourselves too young to think about this terrible subject. The children are not ready yet." Given that most successions take between three and seven years, depending on the complexity of the family and the business, it is better to start too early than a little too late.

10　Celebrate Life.

John and Annie

After a few weeks, Annie calls Mark to schedule the next meeting.

Mark:	*Well, how did this first part go?*
John:	*It was not easy because I am not accustomed to think along those lines. Yet, after brooding on the questions and talking about it with Annie, I must say that it became an interesting exercise.*
Annie:	*It was remarkable to find out that we had a lot of the answers in common and at the same time that we differed on some topics. Discussing these differences was very useful.*
Mark:	*Can you give me an example please.*

Annie:	*On the topic of letting go, I think that, when the time comes, I will just step down from my function. I will shortly start training my most competent collaborator to take over my work.*
John:	*Don't you think it is wise to let her know our plans, even before we talk to the children?*
Annie:	*What do you think, Mark.*
Mark:	*Maybe start the training without talking about succession. This can be a great opportunity to let your collaborator know how much you appreciate her work and that you see a great future for her ahead in the company. Also, this will set an example for other employees who will notice that there is room to grow their career.*
John:	*I realized that stepping down will be much harder for me. I still feel so connected, have so many plans for the future. And besides that, I came to realize that I never did much else besides working. I never took up the golfing thing, too much trouble plus it doesn't add anything besides loosing time, money and the game itself (laughs).*
Mark:	*What did you learn so far?*
John:	*I realize that this process can't be planned like how we do it in our construction business. Not even by using our own construction software (laughs).*
Mark:	*Yes, remember Procrustes?*
John:	*Sure. Anyhow, after all I actually feel proud that we are discussing these topics. The theme of a next step in my, our life and the future of the family@business was something I avoided. I always thought that if you talk to people, even business friends, they would see that as laziness or weakness. How wrong I was!*
Mark:	*Good.*
John:	*Last week I was at the business club and I told one of my friends that we are working on succession. He was immediately very interested and asked a lot of questions. I realize now that many entrepreneurs of our age struggle with these same issues. To realize that we are not alone in this, is a great relief.*
Mark:	*Correct me if I am wrong but do I understand correctly if I say that the both of you are ready to have a meeting with the children?*
John and Annie:	*Full Yes to that. We have decided to have the first meeting without you. After that we would like to introduce you to them. Maybe after that it is useful that you have individual*

Mark:
             conversations with each of them and then again with the whole family.

Mark:
             Perfect proposition. After I will have talked to them, I will suggest how to proceed.

The First Family Meeting

John and Annie invite their children for a Sunday brunch.

Annie: *Dear Children, your father and I have a big announcement today. As parents we are very proud of each and every one of you. You are of course very different and that's OK. We are proud of the way each one of you is finding his own way in life. And, then there is our business. The business is going strong, like you know. The time has come to think of the future. That is why we have consulted with some specialists in the realm of family@business. They will help us make the best possible transition towards the Next Generation, you. This process will need time, discussion and reflection. There is no hurry. But it is complex and delicate. As a family we need to take the first steps. Later on, when we have the beginning of decision for the future, we will involve our loyal management. But for now, it is best that is stays in the family. Before you raise your questions let us toast to the success of our family and business.*

Conclusion

Now that John and Annie took the courageous steps to look inside in order to get an outlook on the future, they desire for themselves, their children, and their life's work, they are ready for the next step: open discussions with the children and later on, with their top management. These steps are the groundwork that lay the foundations for the success of their succession.

The Founders realize that the succession process needs time because it concerns both their management succession and their inheritance succession.

In the next chapters, the family@business consultants will explain the solution-focused approach and how this is effective in dealing with the important issues that every family@business sooner or later faces.

Chapter 8

The Solution-Focused Toolkit

Mark, the Family@business Consultant

Mark's background is both psychology and a business economy. After his studies, he has worked in a university hospital where he got an extensive training in family therapy and other forms of psychotherapy. Coming from a small family@business, Mark has always been fascinated by the dynamics in a family@business. When he first started out working with family businesses, Mark had this remarkable idea that if people are willing to change their life because of emotional and psychological hurt, they sure would be willing to do so because of money and power. This preconception proved to be totally wrong. Mark soon discovered that people from family@businesses are ready for change when they hit upon issues that hamper them in their personal life, in their family interactions, and in the strong connection with the responsibility they feel toward the family@business. Mark learned that very often –metaphorically speaking – the family@business is the eldest child of the family and that most family members, especially of course the "Parents-Founders," go to great lengths in the care for the company. The children literally grow up in the company and are imbibed by the care for it.

The Family@business Is a System

A family best can be understood as one single integrated whole that is different from a group of separate and autonomous individuals (Jaffe, D. 2010). A family is a natural system with its own rules, recurring patterns of behavior, with clearly defined biological and emotional boundaries, and with its own sets of rules of conduct. The family system provides shelter, belonging, and security for its members.

Some families are rather closed to the outside world while others open up easily. According to Dr. Salvador Minuchin, some families are enmeshed and may smother each other while others are more disengaged and have weak ties to each other (Minuchin, S. 1974). Healthy families have balanced

DOI: 10.4324/9781003194200-8

degrees of cohesion and appropriate levels of flexibility so that they can adapt to changing circumstances (Olson, D. 1989).

The *informal rules of conduct* that shape how the family members interact with each other and the world are informal but all too often sticky: "once the eldest son in the family, always the one who feels responsible."

The family system has an unwritten and often unspoken *hierarchy* within which the siblings have different roles and tasks. This family hierarchy – often unconsciously – percolates into the family business. For example, it is often hard for the eldest daughter to take orders in the company from her youngest sister.

At the same time, the business organization also is a system, albeit a man-made system and with a different teleology. The business system is constructed to provide means and meaning to the natural family system.

The great challenge for families in business is to separate the world of the family and the world of the business appropriately and to maintain this separation.

Different Systems Have Different Goals

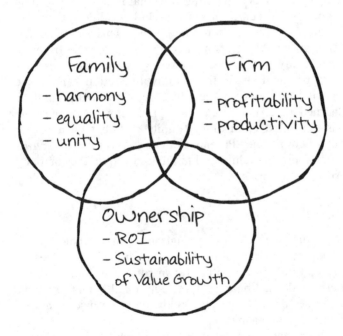

Although not always explicit, every person and every (family or a family@ business) system, has goals in life.

As a *person,* you have goals for yourself, about what it is that you want with and from your life. Dr. Milton H. Erickson, the famous psychiatrist who revolutionized psychotherapy in the fifties and sixties, stated: the purpose in life is to have a long, healthy and prosperous life (Keeney, B. & Erickson, B.A. 2019). For the individual this often is translated as: I want to make a living by doing things that I like, that have added value for others so that this job gives me meaning.

For Founders-Owners, on a personal level, they often started a business themselves because they do not want to work under nor for someone else.

For Founder-Owners, on a business level they want a financial Return on Investment and they often couple this to the wish that the growth of the company is sustainable (in all senses of the word).

A *family* has common goals and it is important to make these family goals explicit, especially when you work with the ones you love. Families strive toward harmony, unity, and equality. These family goals are guidelines for the way the family@business is run.

Last but not least, the *company* also has goals for itself, even if these goals need to be put in words by the humans that make up the company. Company goals often are obvious: being productive in a changing economy, making profit, create meaning for the workers, bring added value to all people involved.

In the center of the Goal Figure, we find the goals that are common to all three systems. The more all three systems have common goals, the more smoothly it goes.

It is unavoidable that the participating systems (individual, family, company) have tension fields and even conflicting goals. E.g. one person in the family demands yearly dividends while another family member wants this profit to be used for corporate investments. Or, the family decides on a business strategy that some family members disagree with.

Founders of the Solution-Focused Approach

Mark was one of the first consultants to adopt and adapt the solution-focused model in working with family@businessses. He had the honor of training with the inventors of the solution-focused model, **Steve de Shazer** and his wife **Insoo Kim Berg**. Afterward, he invited them regularly to give seminars and workshops that gave him the opportunity to hone his skills in this approach. Since Steve and Insoo were psychotherapists, Mark had to translate and adapt the solution-focused approach so that it became a useful tool for application in management and coaching for the family@business. He wrote two books and several articles on the topic. His publications are instruments that Mark uses when working with his clients.

The Solution-Focused Consultants Meet Up

After the meetings with John and Annie and their children, the first steps toward the succession process are put in place. Mark contacts his colleague Prof. Cynthia Hange and they come forward with the next steps. They agree that Prof. C. Hange will take care of the more theoretical background so that the family gets all the necessary information they need. Mark will take the lead in the family meetings and coach the discussions toward efficacy.

Nothing Is More Practical Than a Good Theory

From here on, you will witness a conversation between the consultants in which they discuss central solution-focused themes:

- the importance of a good working relationship between consultants and clients;
- the need to avoid triangulation;
- the importance of asking questions instead of telling people what to do;
- the three mandates that are so essential when working as family@ business consultants;
- the theme of resource orientation that is the essence of the solution-focused approach;
- the seven premises upon which the evidence-based solution-focused model is based.

Instead of describing the insights that underpin solution-focused thinking and working in a theoretical way, we invite you to discover them for yourself by participating in the lively conversations between the two experts.

If you're learning style is more structured, you could construct (and write down for yourself) a more formal approach from the ideas embedded in the conversations.

The Importance of a Good Working Relationship

Mark: *It is an honor to work with you on this dossier, professor.*
Cynthia: *Likewise. Please call me Cynthia; the "professor" is for my students.*

Mark: I am happy that we meet so that we can get to know each other.
Cynthia: Likewise. I deem it important to be on the same wavelength when working with colleagues in family@business cases.
Mark: Indeed. When everything runs smoothly, consultants can easily work alongside of each other. The same goes for our work with the family.

Avoid Triangularization

Mark: But from both our experiences, we know that when the going gets tough, we really need to coordinate our efforts.
Cynthia: I agree. Otherwise we run the risk of getting "triangularized."
Mark: Please explain.
Cynthia: Well, we get in a triangle: you, myself and one or more of the family members.
Mark: Like when for example, two of the kids have a different opinion of each other and they seek alliances with one of us. If we don't act in a coordinated manner, we might end up favoring one or the other, or at least give them that impression. Or worse, we might get stuck in different opinions that are not constructive for the case.
Cynthia: Exactly. There are many such examples. As a matter of fact, once the process of the succession gets into choppy waters and the real knots have to be cut, stress and pressure will descend upon the family members.
Mark: And when that happens, and we both know from experience that this will happen, family members might feel the tendency to seek backup from the consultants for their own viewpoint.
Cynthia: Correct. And this is not a matter of "if" disagreements happen but more of "when" disagreements will happen. Then we need to pull together and not allow us to be torn by their disagreements.
Mark: And we have to avoid taking sides. Our job is not about information nor is it about who is right or who is wrong. Our job is about...
Cynthia: Transformation! As family@business consultants, we always work with the working relationships between the parties involved. That way we stay neutral and work only for the good of the company and never for the good of one family member.
Mark: instead of getting caught in a triangle, we keep working in a T:

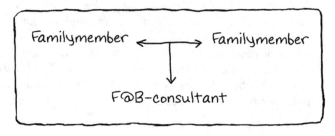

Cynthia:	Plus, we need to keep our ego in check.
Mark (smiling):	Yes, not one of us has an ego issue but all the other family@business consultants have one (both laugh). As you know, I already had long conversations with both the parents and with all of the children. They are very cooperative. Of course, there are issues that need work.
Cynthia:	Sure, that is why we, family@business consultants were invented in the first place (both laugh). Probably you already know that I did a Leadership workshop with Eric and Ella, Cherly was not ready to participate at that moment.
Mark:	Cherly told me that she came to see you and that she did the exercise with you personally. As a matter of fact, she told me she did the exercise twice.
Cynthia:	That surprises me that she told you. I would have thought she was not ready for it. But, yes. She did the exercise twice and I must say there is potential within her.
Mark:	indeed, there is. Cherly even told me that she would ask her direct boss, Alice, to give her more challenging jobs.
Cynthia:	So, she can show results to her Daddy? A classic.
Mark:	A classic indeed but probably a very valuable step forward for Cherly.
Cynthia:	I gave a workshop for the siblings on leadership indicators and gave them an exercise that they can use to both monitor and hone their leadership skills.
Mark:	I read about your 10 indicators in your book but I particularly like your idea of asking questions so that the clients need to find out for themselves.

Solution-Focused Questions

| Cynthia: | From my experience asking questions, even suggestive questions, is more effective than just lecturing. |
| Mark: | So true. If you ask someone a question, the law of linguistics obliges that person to answer and most importantly, the person who answers a question becomes the owner of the answer. This insight helped me become a far better family@business consultant than I was in the beginning when I thought that I should know it all or at least know better than my clients. In my early days as family@business consultant I acted more like an advisor: "dear clients, sit and listen, I am now going to tell you how you need to live and work." It was very hard work because I needed to convince people. When I met them a few weeks after, they just forgot what we talked about so it was not only very tiring and even tiresome but also very ineffective. |

Cynthia: *Still we, as professionals need to know more as to fill up our management mandate. Nowadays one can sometimes hear the mantra "the client is the expert of his/her own life." I am convinced that this mantra often is misunderstood in the sense that the client has all the answers and that the coach is just there to help the client discover what he/she already knows. This leads nowhere. I personally rather believe in: "the client together with the family@business professional create the expertise the family and the company need in order to move forward." Our professional expertise and knowledge complement the contribution of the family members. Of course, later in the process we will make room for all the other stakeholders like the non-family management, employees and other relevant parties.*

The Three Mandates

Mark: *I totally agree. As family@business consultants, we always have three mandates. These mandates are always and at the same time operational. Depending on each situation, one of the mandates is in the foreground while the others are more in the background.*

First allow me to explain the different mandates.

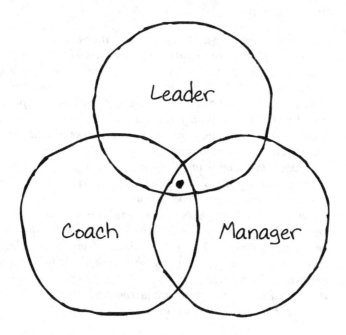

The Mandate As a Leader

Mark: *We have a leadership mandate, meaning that we, the professionals, take the lead in the intervention. We decide which questions we ask, which answers we follow up and which answer we leave aside. We decide whom we invite, in what order. For example, in our John and Annie family@business case, the parents invited us. We talked to the parents first, and then set up a meeting with the whole family and after that, we had our first individual interviews. We did not talk to their management, employees yet. Those meetings are for later. In order to create no misunderstanding: leadership has nothing to do with being bossy, on the contrary. Leadership is what it says: taking the lead. By the way, you can only offer leadership to people who want to follow you.*

Cynthia: *So, leadership is not a given but leadership must be earned in the eyes of those who follow you?*

Mark: *Yes. The simple question: "Correct me if I am wrong. Do I understand you correctly when you say X?" is an application of this principle. In technical terms, the leadership mandate is bi-directional.*

Cynthia: *With this question you take leadership by inviting the client to take leadership: clever.*

The Coaching Mandate

Mark: *Our second mandate is the mandate as a coach. In our solution-focused approach to family@business, coaching is defined as creating the context in which we help the family@business to reach their goals by using their own possibilities and resources.*

Cynthia: *That is a different position than the expert-consultant position. I can already feel that what you are about to tell me is going to have impact on the terminology. Family@business consultant might become coach or something else.*

Mark: *We coach the family members and their teams throughout the transformation process. One could say that a successful family@ business consultant is a "coachultant."*

Cynthia: *Great neologism. What about the term "trusted advisor"?*

Mark: *Obviously, I am aware that this term is often used in the literature on family@business. Yet, I have always found it a bit peculiar, trusted advisor. Why would you work with an advisor that you do not trust? (Both laugh).*

Cynthia: *At the end of the day, these are just words.*

Mark: *Correct, but then again, our work is words!*

Cynthia: *So, you explained the leadership mandate and the coaching mandate. There is one left.*

The Mandate as Process Manager, Part 1

Mark: *That is what we call the mandate as a "manager," although the word "manager" is not precise enough and overused in an organizational context. Maybe, the word "steward" is more appropriate: one that has charge of something or someone.*

Cynthia: *Why not make it simple and use the term "process manager"?*

Mark: *Good idea. The process manager mandate has two parts in it. First there is our professional expertise, knowledge and experience. We still are supposed to be experts in our field although our field is very broad, ranging from basic legal and fiscal knowledge over expertise in business strategies to psychological and relationship skills and family dynamics. On top of this, we have experience with helping family@businessses through the complex process of succession. We know, or at least we should know, more about the in-and-outs, the do's-and-don'ts, about possible pitfalls and ways to avoid them or at least get out of them quickly, about what works best both on a business level, a personal level, and the family level.*

T.E.A.M

Cynthia: *That is why it is so important to work as a team when dealing with family@business issues.*

Mark: *You as the professor of management and myself as the psychologist indeed work together as a team whereby T.E.A.M. stands for Together Each Achieves More.*

The Mandate As Process Manager, Part 2

Mark: *The second part of our process manager mandate is the fact that we make agreements with everybody involved. The law of efficacy says to keep it simple: do as you say and say as you do.*

Cynthia: *Let me try to recap what you just told me. That way I make sure I really understand it. In working with a family@business, we have three mandates at the same time. So, it is and-and-and.*

We must choose in which circumstances we put one of the mandates on the foreground while the other two stay present in the background. Using our leadership mandate, we take the lead of the consulting process. In our mandate as a coach we set the context in which we help our clients to again help themselves to obtain their goals by making use of their resources. Whenever possible, we help them to help each other to do so. This concerns all parties involved: both family as well as all stakeholders in the system around the family@business. And in our third mandate, we apply our professional expertise; we make agreements with our clients and make sure the terms of these agreements are met. By rotating between the three mandates, our intervention both follows and directs the continuous dynamic of the consulting process.

Mark: *That gives you 10/10 on an exam. (Both laugh)*

Up and Downsizing

Cynthia: *Can I offer you a suggestion?*

Mark: *Be my guest.*

Cynthia: *Maybe the power of this three-mandate tool is not only in the rotating of the mandates. Maybe one could visualize the mandates becoming smaller or larger in certain situations. For example, the leadership mandate of the Chairman of the Board of Directors is larger than her process management mandate. Or another example, the coaching mandate of a team leader is larger than his mandate as a process manager. From working with large family@businessses that e.g. are in G4 or G5, I know that some of those CEOs hardly ever spent time on their process mandate, meaning they only descend on the floor for supporting people and refrain from operational issues. One of them told me: "My main task is to offer leadership to the extended family and coaching them. I haven't taken an operational decision on my own for many years now. That is simply not my job. Others are far better equipped to do that work than me." This person's leadership mandate is far bigger than the other two. It might look like this:*

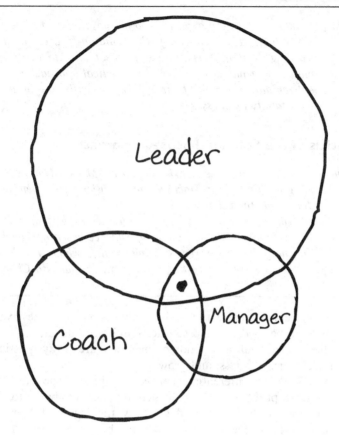

Mark: *That is a useful addition, Cynthia, thank you.*

Cynthia: *We should share this material with the family, don't you think?*

Mark: *Sure. And we will. Oh, and by the way, before I forget, just like the leadership mandate needs to be earned, so it is for the coaching mandate. You can only coach people if they choose to be coached by you.*

Cynthia: *Your position as a leader and as a coach is never a given but must always be earned.*

Mark: *Your mandate as process manager, well, that is a given. You are supposed to have the professional expertise this job requires. Just like you are supposed to do what you say and say what you do.*

Cynthia: *In my opinion, the three-mandate-tool can be applied in many circumstances.*

Mark: *Sure. It can be used when you are a line manager, a director, a team leader, and a self-employed professional coach. Wherever one works with people, there's always room for leadership, for coaching and for managing the process.*

Cynthia: *I am sure it is even applicable to my position as a professor.*

Mark: *No doubt. The beauty of the solution-focused thinking and working is that it is more a mindset and an attitude than a bunch of techniques. It is a very practical approach with a sound epistemology behind it. It is pre-eminently useful in working with family businesses.*

Essentials of the Solution-Focused Approach

Cynthia: *Could you give me a brief synopsis, Mark? That will help me integrate the solution-focused approach in my interventions for the John and Annie Family.*

Mark: *My pleasure, Cynthia. Here comes a synopsis of the solution-focused model. This, by the way, evidence-based[1] approach is based on the following seven starting points, which I will explicate further on. (see the rest of this Chapter 8 and also Chapter 9)*

---

1   Every person, family and business always has resources available that can be used to build solutions and reach its goals.

2   However difficult a situation seems, there are always possibilities for change, progress, and growth.

3   It is KEY to differentiate between problems/issues and limitations. A problem/issue is defined by the possibility to find a solution. A limitation is defined by the fact that there is no solution thinkable, but it just needs to be accepted for what it is. How to deal with the consequences of a limitation is a problem.

4   Problems are golden signposts to possible solutions as seen in Formula P (see Chapter 6).

5   Goal Orientation: The question "what do you want instead" is more powerful than the question "why."

6   The relationship between all parties involved is the motor for change and growth.

7   Trust, respect, and hope are essential in working with the ones you love.

The Solution-Focused Consultants Continue

Mark: *I especially like the first premise. Like Insoo Kim Berg, one of the founders, always taught us: "always approach the client in his or her resources first."*

Cynthia: *Exactly. I also prefer to work from this standpoint. It makes the conversations with the clients so much lighter, more enjoyable and at the same time more effective. We are of course all trained to look for the root causes behind the problems and this solution-focused approach offers such an elegant alternative when working with people, behavior and emotions.*

Mark: *The search for the root cause hidden behind or even in the problem is only effective for more mechanical problems.*

Cynthia: *Correct. But we don't deal with mechanical problems. We deal with people.*

Mark: *The nicest thing about the solution focused approach, for me at least, is the given that one can use this "technology for change" in an almost invisible manner. You don't need to be explicit about it towards clients. It is just another form of conversation, with different accents and different focus points.*

Cynthia: *As a matter of fact, I remember Steve de Shazer, Insoo Kim Berg's husband and cofounder of the solution-focused approach, saying about psychotherapy: "it is just a conversation." Same goes for family@business sessions, they are just conversations where the solution-focused thinking-behind-the-thinking is kept implicit. You can ask the clients if they are interested in the background of how you work. My experience is that most of them are friendly and say yes to that question. But very soon you will find out that their attention slips away and that they just want you to help them, not lecture them. That's fine because our job is to help them help themselves.*

Resource Orientation

Mark: *Yes, help them to use their own resources, strong points, things that still work in spite of their problems (or challenges ☺).*

Cynthia: *Mark, how would you define a resource?*

Mark: *For me a resource is whatever the client can use to help him or her obtain their goals. That can be anything, but it is important to keep in mind that a resource is not something that "is" like an object. I'll give you an example. Imagine that your boss, the Dean of your faculty sends you an email: "Dear Cynthia, would you be so kind as to prepare the business model for the next academic year for your faculty. Sorry that I am so late with this request, but the meeting is already in two days. Good luck." The fact that you only have two days to prepare such an important memo is a resource.*

Cynthia: *sorry but...HUH?*

Mark: Well, the little time you are allowed obliges you to be as concise and precise as possible without bothering with too much detail.

Cynthia: I see.

Mark: Now imagine that your Dean sends you another mail, instead, this time the message is: "Dear Cynthia, would you be so kind as to prepare the business model for your faculty for next academic year. The faculty meeting where we will discuss this is next month." The fact that you have six weeks is a resource because it allows you to prepare this memo with all the whistles and bells thinkable. So, having both little and lots of time is a resource depending on how you use the time. More time is not necessarily a bigger resource than less time. It is about how you use the time given.

Positive Thinking Is for Gurus

Cynthia: Great example, now I fully understand. Solution-focused thinking is something entirely different from positive thinking.

Mark: Sure. Positive thinking is reserved for holistic gurus who pretend that when you think about life in a positive manner, everything always will be OK. Quod non! Solution-focused thinking is seeing your half-empty bottle of water as half full. There is the same amount of reality in each bottle but when you are lost in a desert, it is better for your survival rate to see the reality in your bottle as half full.

Cynthia: so, Focused thinking is pragmatic realism?

Mark: Yep! The solution-focused model actually is an alternative epistemology by which our clients and we co-create a different reality.

Cynthia (laughing):   Now who is the professor here?

Mark: You are! May I add one more element that is crucial in the solution-focused approach in working with family@ businessses?

Cynthia: Sure.

Mark: First, allow me a little story. Many years ago, Steve de Shazer and I were enjoying a beer after a workshop. We were shooting the breeze and talking about everything and nothing. You know how that goes. We were talking about a famous colleague - I will not mention his name- when Steve said: "X is like the ocean, deep, ever moving but going nowhere." After some laughs, it struck me. A conversation without a goal is like the ocean. A family@ business intervention that does not works towards the goals of the family or the business is deep, ever moving, high on billable hours but goes nowhere. In contrast to this, the Solution Focused approach is goal oriented.

Goal Orientation

Cynthia: Don't you think we have to be careful with the words "goal oriented"? This might be misinterpreted as "If I push her, Doctor, it hurts there. What do I have to do? Doctor: stop pushing."

Mark: Absolutely. That is not what we mean by goal orientation at all. It is much more complex. First, we always ask the family what it is that they want to talk about so that our cooperation will be useful for them and their company. Second, we use our three mandates to coach when possible but also direct when necessary for the simple reason that G1 and G2 have no experience in the succession process and therefore need some coaching. Third, the goals of a family@business are much broader than just money things.

Cynthia: Indeed. The younger generations are focused on Quintuple P's: Passion, Pleasure, Planet, People and- as the last, Profit. I have the impression that they see Profit as a means to an end for the other P's.

Mark: Adding meaningfulness for all stakeholders, a term we will have to talk more about later is an important goal. And that surpasses the mere money thing.

Cynthia: Correct.

Mark: This being said, don't you think the time has come to organize meetings with the Siblings? You can offer them information about which tools they can use to prepare themselves for their future in or outside the family@business.

Cynthia: And then you, Mark, can invite them into exercises that will prepare them for whatever decision they will take. After all, even if they will take different positions in the family@business or even outside of it, like Ella, they still are the next generation of owners. This step will help them get insight in the difference between the management and the ownership of the company.

Armed with the solution-focused toolkit, the next chapter will teach you what to do in the working relationship with your family@business clients

Note

1 See Addendum 2. Is the solution-focused approach an evidence-based model? YES!

Chapter 9

The Solution Tango

Protocol-Based Methodical Working Models

Classic coaching and management models often use a well-defined script, a protocol that consists of different steps and they demand of its users that they methodically follow the different steps in the protocol. Such a methodic approach is useful when it comes to more technical interventions. Imagine you are sitting in an airplane and the pilot has forgotten to shut down his intercom. You hear the pilot telling his co-pilot: "you know, my dear co-pilot, I feel so creative today and I am fed up with all these boring safety procedures. Just check if the landing gear functions as it should and then the rest probably is OK too." If you hear this, our strong advice is to do something illegal like smoking on the toilet in order to make sure that you get off that plane a.s.a.p. Protocol-based methodical models are useful when dealing with things like safety measures, interventions following a fire, and other accidents, evacuation protocols, etc.

When it comes to leadership, management, and coaching these predetermined steps tend to initialize inflexibility.

A Client-Centered Approach

The solution-focused approaches this differently. All attention is concentrated on this particular client in this particular context. The client can be an individual, a family, an organization like a business, a management team, or the family@business as a whole. As a matter of fact, when you read the word "client" in this book, the word actually means "the client in his relevant context." Metaphorically speaking, the solution-focused approach crafts a fresh model for each client situation, meaning an approach that fits the goals, the needs, and the possibilities of this particular client in this context.

DOI: 10.4324/9781003194200-9

The Solution-Focused Interview

Because one never knows in advance what clients will do or say, Mark realizes that it is useless to work with fixed scripts to structure your sessions. He learned that it is far better to improvise on the themes that the client brings up. Of course, Mark has a loose structure in mind, more like a tango. That way he can direct the conversation so that he both gets the information he needs as well as he puts the client to work. The essence of solution-focused coaching for family@business is not getting the information for the mere sake of knowing it but putting the information to work for sparking the necessary transformation.

Infinite Possibilities

Like in the real tango, there is a limited number of steps but the possible combinations are unlimited. In our Solution Tango, these steps are danced with the clients in the context of their family, personality, and the dynamics of their family@business in the changing economic circumstances.

The order in which you use the steps of the solution-focused dance is purely decided by what seems most useful at that particular moment. Sometimes, you only use few steps, but you can also use all of them or combine some of them. It is even possible that you retreat your steps and go back to previous steps. In that sense, you can dance backward in order to make progress.

The Solution Tango[1]

What exactly is it that you do in the contact with your interlocutors, be it clients, family members, co-workers, or staff? Instead of using a fixed interactional protocol, you dance with your interlocutors. The five steps of the Solution Tango structure the pattern of interactions between the family@business consultant and the client(s). This is equally true when you use the Solution Tango in working with your employees. The five steps shape the process of the interaction, and by process we mean the form of the interaction and not it's content. The content of the conversation comes from the client's situation and is related to his goals for the intervention.

For didactic reasons, we present the five steps in logical order. However, this order serves only as an aide-mémoire. In reality, as you will see in the next chapter, the only fixed step is the invitation to the dance (by which you establish a working relationship), which always comes first (or you would not have a dancing partner and therefore no dance). The order of the steps after step number 1, depends on the situation (the issues, your partners, the circumstances, what it is that you want to accomplish during that particular meeting, etc.). And yet, the ensuing order of the steps is not random. Your solution-focused dance movements are more like an elegant tango than like hopping around in a random manner.

In the next chapter, you will see how the Solution Tango is danced in real life when you read the conversations with the siblings. For now, we teach you the basic steps.

Music, Maestro!

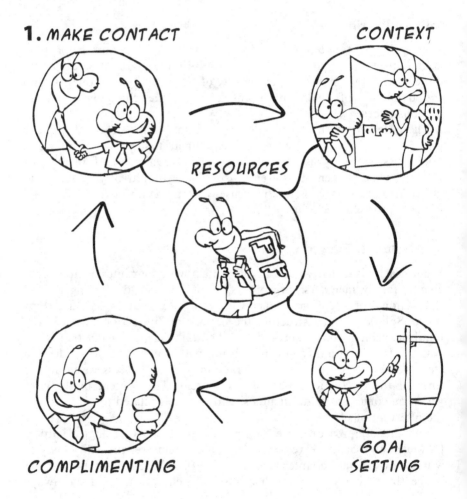

1. *MAKE CONTACT*

CONTEXT

RESOURCES

GOAL SETTING

COMPLIMENTING

Step I Contact is the motor for change

1. MAKE CONTACT

When you work with the ones you love and/or when you work for a long time with the same people, you might get the impression that making contact is not so necessary, that contact is self-evident. This impression simply is wrong. You want proof? Imagine what the atmosphere in your home would be like if everybody in the household suddenly decides that it is no longer necessary to say hello to each other because you have been a family for so long.

That is why you see the number 1 in the figure: contact is always the very first step you start with. In fact, contact is the motor of change.

This is as simple to do as it is to forget to do it. Making contact is easy: you start by being friendly and attentive to the others.

The purpose of making contact is to create an optimal working relationship. This implies reaching out to others by making sure that your clients, colleagues, and staff feel that you are interested in them and that you value them both as a person and as a client/colleague/staff. Making contact can start with shaking hands, saying hello, asking and remembering personal things about the other, remembering and reminding people of specific details that show that you make the effort to remember. There are myriad ways of making contact, just pick the ones that suit you the best, and that you feel comfortable with.

The benefits of creating and maintaining a good contact are multiple. For starters, most people prefer to have a good time at work because it is more enjoyable to work in a positive atmosphere. This does not mean that you are partying all day but it sure means profit in all possible meanings of the word and for everybody involved. Secondly, if you have a good relationship with the others, they will allow you more room for mistakes. Third, and if you are in a leadership position, maybe most important, when you fall on hard times and tough decisions need to be made that require difficult changes, a good working relationship will make it easier to move into a constructive direction.

Step 2 Clarifying the context

CONTEXT

Nothing in life works in a vacuum. Nobody in a family@business works in a vacuum.

When you are working with the ones you love and/or you work in the same organization for a longer time, you might get the impression that asking questions to clarify the context is not necessary. This impression – again – is simply wrong. Why? If you do not do the hard work of asking questions, you treat your own assumptions about the situation as the one and only reality. It is a strange paradox in corporate life that you work together with people on a daily basis and tend to think that you know them like you know yourself whereas you often haven't got a clue as to who they really are as (private) individuals. This paradox is even stronger in a family@business. Because of the Familyness, it is all too often assumed that the family members know each other through and through. But there is only one constant in life and that is change. Plus, by the time the siblings start working in the company, they have gone their own way in life for some time.

Mark, our family@business consultant, has some information about the children because he talked about them with John and Annie. Yet it is important not to allow yourself to get caught up in prejudices that inevitably are formed whenever you talk about someone. So, Mark often uses what he calls a context-clarifying question. This question is both simple and profound because it shows the one you are talking to that you are more interested in who he/she is as a person than in his problems or the underlying reasons.

Although adapted to every situation, this question basically goes as follows: "would you be so kind as to tell me something about yourself. How old are you? Do you have a relationship? What kind of studies are you doing or have you done? What kind of work do you do? What is your role and position in the family@business?"

This basic context-clarifying question can be varied upon according to the situation. Let us give some examples.

Imagine you are a manager that is new to this team, then you can ask them: "Dear All, since I am new, I would like to get to know you as a team. Can you tell me something about yourself? How long do you work here, what is your responsibility in the team?"

Now imagine you are a team leader that works for some time with the same team. Then you might ask: "Dear Colleagues, we work together for quite some time. We recently made a big strategic change and went through a re-organization in our company. How will that affect your functioning? What will you need to do differently in the near future? How will that affect our way of cooperating?"

Step 3 *Goal setting*

GOAL
SETTING

Setting the right goals and finding ways to help your clients or staff to set the right goals is a crucial task for a leader, manager, and coach. Goals are the signposts that direct the work you do together. Clear, concrete, and realistic goals that are relevant to everybody involved, including the family@business as a whole, lead your interventions to swift and lasting results.

The basic goal-setting question is: "What do we need to talk about so that this conversation will be useful to you?" The basic goal-setting question can be adapted to the specific situation. Let us give you some examples.

Imagine you are the team leader and you want to make your meetings more useful, you can open each meeting with: "what do we need to talk about as a team in the coming hour so that our meeting will be useful for all of us and for the company?" Beware: if you use this question, your meeting probably is going to be a lot shorter. And you will quickly find out which meetings you can just cancel because nothing useful comes out of them anyway.

Imagine you are the CEO and in the meeting with your top management you ask: "what do we need to talk about so that our clients will benefit from the outcome of our meeting?"

Or, specified to a family@business that e.g. works on its succession: "what needs to happen in the coming months so that working on this succession planning process will be useful to you, the family, and the business?"

In knowledge-driven companies, goal setting is an interactive process that you do together with all parties involved. (When one works at a conveyor belt, the goal is set for you and you just have to follow the rhythm that it is set to.) In Chapter 7 you learned the three solution-focused mandates. Now the time has come to set them to work. When working with professional knowledge-workers, it is the leader that sets the initial goals and aligns them with the goals of the business. But the leader needs to coach his staff so that they buy into these goals. And then, as a team, you set the managerial milestones toward the goals and, together, you clarify which results are wanted. The only thing left to do then is: plan, do and trust your professionals that you judge by their results.

Goal setting is an incremental activity that does not happen in a single shot. On the contrary, goal setting is a continuous process. Every time a (partial) goal is obtained or failed, the next line of goals is adapted according to this new information. This idea of goal-setting as a continuous process is important because it helps us not to fall into the trap of thinking that once a goal is set, it's there to stay forever. Business life is too volatile, and we need to be optimally flexible. This is what Charles Darwin meant when he talked about the survival of the fittest. You have to change so that you fit with the constantly changing circumstances.

If you want to "minimax": obtain maximum results with minimum effort, we recommend that you use the following criteria when setting goals. (if, however, for some obscure reasons, you prefer maximum effort with minimal results, feel free to do the opposite ☺)

Useful goals have the following characteristics:

1.   Useful goals are realistic and achievable
      This point is fairly obvious. However, in business it is all too often overlooked. The myth of "more is better," "the harder to get, the better" are a good way to overstretch yourself and others. In the solution-focused approach, we opt for ambitious goals that can be

reached with the resources of the company. Why try and bring down the moon when you can work on good quarterly results?

2.   Useful goals can be described in terms of observable behavior

When goals are not translated into concrete, clearly defined and visible behaviors, they remain vague and unclear. Consider these goals: "You should work harder," "You must be more motivated," "Try to get your results faster," "Strive for more cooperation in your team," and, "Loosen up in your social contacts." These goals are vague because everybody will have his or her own interpretation of what "working harder" or "being more motivated" etc. means. This often leads to time-consuming debates about the how and when of what should be achieved. It is easy to see why such goals are hard to achieve – you have no clearly visible sign that tells you when you have reached them. In such situations, it can seem like it is up to the whim of the boss whether something is rated OK or not!

If you translate these goals into exact and observable behavior, it becomes much easier to be successful in reaching them as progress can be measured. "Be on time" turns into "Start at eight o'clock." "If necessary, work overtime to finish that project" turns into "Go home when the job is done. Make sure to finalize that project by the end of this week." "Loosen up at the office" becomes "When you enter your office, say good morning to everybody, and go out for lunch with your colleagues." When goals are stated in terms of concrete desired behavior, it is much easier to know what one should be striving for. These behaviors act like signposts on your way to the goal. Stated simply, the more concretely you describe your goals – "What do I want to be doing to obtain my goals? What do others need to see me doing?" the easier the road to achievement becomes.

3.   Useful goals start small and grow bigger

Success breeds success. Setting a string of small consecutive goals toward your bigger goal makes it easier to achieve the big goal. Taking small steps instead of giant leaps is often the most useful and reliable way to get what you want. Small victories create an ideal breeding ground for further and bigger successes.

Here, too, questions come in handy: "what would be the smallest step forward?" "what is the first sign that will tell us that our project moves in the right direction?"

Step 4 Un-covering resources

RESOURCES

The resource orientation lies at the heart of the solution-oriented approach and is therefore drawn as the hub of the wheel of change.

The solution-focused model starts out from the assumption that every human system, be it an individual or a team, has resources at its disposal at all times, even in times of trouble! When problems occur, we see it as an indication that the concerned parties in the problem have momentarily lost confidence in their own solution-focused possibilities, simply because they have lost the access to their own resources. You might say that they have (temporarily) lost their personal manual on "how to use our resources."

The job of the solution-building manager is to help his or her staff (re) discover their "forgotten" resources and/or to give them new tools for building solutions. In this context, we define "resources" as "every available tool that can be used to create solutions." Resources can be very intangible, such as effort, motivation, loyalty to the company, team spirit, or expertise, but they also can be very concrete tools, such as communication skills, crisis and conflict management skills, procedures, business insights, technical tools, time, money, or attention. Sometimes what initially seems negative can be considered a positive thing. A crisis can become an opportunity – a setback in business opens your eyes, losing clients may prompt you to pay more attention to them, complaints may encourage you to become more customer-oriented. In short, your company's weaknesses may be turned into opportunities for improvement, and threats can turn into chances.

The key concept is the resource orientation. Experience, expertise, talents, skills, environmental factors, and coincidental lucky breaks are what they are, but they become resources the moment you learn to actually use them to achieve something. Although it contains the same reality, learning to see a half-empty bottle as a half-full one is more useful for your survival. Resources can be discovered or more precisely, uncovered by asking the right questions. Questions that come in handy are: "what is still working in spite of the problems? What would you like to keep doing because it works so well for you in your job? What are the things that you, your siblings, your parents, your staff, your family@business as a whole is doing so well that you want to keep doing that?"

In several places in this book, you have already encountered the concept of resources and there is much more to come!

Step 5 Complimenting

COMPLIMENTING

What do you do with the resources that you dis- and/or uncovered in your clients/staff/family members? You applaud the person and his resources by giving compliments. The purpose of giving compliments is to show your interlocutor that you appreciate their contributions and that you endorse their useful resources because these are instrumental for building solutions toward the goals. Your appreciation will enhance your working relationship in a positive way, boost your client/staff's confidence, shift the attention from the problem to a possible solution and encourage the client to do more of what actually works.

Compliments are used to reinforce aspects of your interlocutor's behavior that you would like to see happening more often. It is actually very simple: if an employee does something useful that is beneficial to him- or herself, the team, and the company, give them a compliment on it. "Thanks for staying late and helping your colleague out when his planning program crashed yesterday. Without your expert knowledge of the system he would certainly not have been able to get production planning running by the time the factory started up early this morning. Congratulations on your expertise and team spirit." A compliment can be about anything useful – on someone's good memos, clear information, sharp analysis of a certain case, punctuality (or, if the person is habitually late, conscientiousness in always letting you know), firm convictions (or open-mindedness), etc.

The Formula G-R-C

Giving compliments, showing appreciation, and recognition for the other's efforts are the universal currency in human interactions.

Compliments always work on two stringent conditions:

1. that you mean what you say
    This is straightforward: not being authentic when giving a compliment is counterproductive. So, if you don't mean what you say, it is better to shut up.
2. that the compliment is relevant

A relevant compliment is a compliment that you give on those resources of your interlocutor that he can use to obtain his goals. So, here is a direct link with step 3 goal setting. Without goals to orient your compliments, your compliments don't carry much power. It is like – in the midst of a board meeting – telling your CFO that you appreciate that he polished his shoes. Yes, this is friendly. But no, it carries no power because his nicely polished shoes are rather irrelevant for the goal of his contribution to the meeting.

However, when the goal of the meeting is to share an in-depth analysis of the financial situation and your CFO has delivered a detailed yet a for non-financial experts fully comprehensible presentation, the following compliment is relevant: "Dear CFO, what a great presentation. The board wanted to know the ins and outs of the financial situation and your presentation was spot on. We really appreciate that you not only showed us a clear overview in your power-point presentation. You gave us a detailed document in which we can study the underlying numbers. And you explained your material in terms that even I could understand. Great job!"

Hence the formula G-R-C. The power lies in the connection of the compliments to those, and only those, resources that are needed to reach the goals.

When there is no goal, giving compliments is merely being friendly (which in itself already work better than acting grumpy).

When you can't find resources within your interlocutor and his context, you should buy "resource-detecting-glasses."

When you can't formulate a compliment toward the other, you shouldn't be surprised if your working relationships are on the sour side.

Mark: Cynthia, provided you keep it to yourself, I have a secret to tell you. The solution-oriented approach is a perfect tool for lazy consultants. (Both laugh) Solution-focused practitioners like to "minimax,": we like to provoke maximum results for our customers while we put minimal energy into it ourselves. In order to do this, we designed the Formula G-R-C.

Cynthia: Let me guess. G-R-C stands for Goal, Resources and Compliments.

Mark: Correct. In the classic solution focused approach, I often hear people say: the more compliments, the better. I do not agree with this. Imagine,

Cynthia, that tomorrow at your university, everybody starts complimenting you all day long about whatever. What would that do to you?

Cynthia: You don't want to know! (laughs)

Mark: Indeed. No, in our approach we say: the less compliments, the
better, on the condition that the compliments you give are relevant.
Compliments are relevant when given on those resources that
the clients can use to obtain their goals. Hence, the power of
combination that is expressed in the formula G-R-C.

Cynthia: Can you give me an example, please.

Mark: Sure, Cynthia. I know that besides your academic work, your goal
is to help family@business people as much you can by developing
interesting and challenging tools for them. I really like the way you
developed those ten Indicators of Leadership Potential. I want to
compliment you with how you translated them into a dynamic
instrument that suits and services your family@business clients.

Cynthia: Oh, well, thank you. That is very nice of you.

Mark: See? G-R-C. (both laugh)

The Solution-Focused Consultants

Cynthia: Great aide-mémoire, this five steps dance. It is simple, easy to
understand and to remember. At the same time, it is not a protocol,
no fixed order.

Mark: It is always the best to use the step 1, making contact, first. But that
is just common sense.

Cynthia: Common sense, yes but often forgotten.

Mark: I explained the 5 steps in their didactic logic. In reality one doesn't
necessarily uses all the 5 steps in one conversation. And like in the
real tango, you can dance backwards in order to make progress.

In the next chapter, we will demonstrate how this 5-step Solution Tango
works in practice in the interaction between the siblings.

Note

1 The solution-focused approach to management and coaching is explained in
great detail in our book "The Solution Tango" (Cauffman, L. Cyan Books 2006).

Chapter 10

Conversations with the Siblings

Stories of family feuds are good sellers of books, magazines, and newspapers. Even the general public loves to read about the spectacular: about the murder within the famous Gucci family, about the two decades of open warfare between the Ambani brothers from India's giant multinational Reliance, about the Dassler brothers that created Adidas versus Puma, the list goes on and on. If your curiosity peaks, just type "Family Business feuds" in Google and have a field day.

Yet these stories are exceptions. The absolute majority of family@business just go about their business in a normal, unspectacular, and – in the eyes of some – sometimes even boring manner. Normal means of course that family@business families, besides being happy and living a life of contentment, also go through the dark sides of life: ill-luck, sickness, emotional crises, disappointments in each other and the world, divorce, jealousy, etc. Yet all of those dark(er) things are part of normal life. Pretending that the lives of the family in family@businesses are fairy tales of financial success, eternal happiness, and total mutual understanding is reserved for naïve believers in a perfect world.

Reality is so much more interesting!

The Genogram

After John and Annie had their first formal meeting with the children, an appointment was made for them to have a talk with Mark, the family@ business consultant.

Mark has two very useful tools at hand when he starts working with a family@business: The Genogram and the Three Circle Model by Tagiuri and Davis. This last model comes in handy when working with the family@ business organization, especially when the succession plan comes into a later stage (we will deal with this model in Chapter 14 where we explain solution-focused stakeholder stewardship).

The Genogram[1] is a pictorial display of family relations that offers a quick oversight of everybody involved. As more than one generation enters

DOI: 10.4324/9781003194200-10

the family business, and certainly if different family branches are involved, this is necessary to maintain the overview.

The John and Annie Family

As we already know, by the time this meeting takes place, John is 57, Annie 56, Eric 32, Ella 27, and Cherly is 24 years old.

Eric is married to Lars and they have two adopted children, Esther, 5 and John Jr., 2. Ella is in a steady relationship with her friend Max, preparing to become a neurologist, but because of their complicated work schedules in different hospitals over the country, they do not live together. Cherly is single for the moment but she was engaged to Jeff, the son of a former employee.

In a genogram this looks like this:

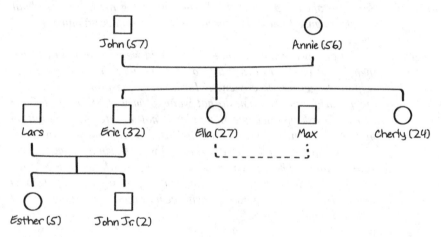

The Sibling Interviews

Let's see how this Solution Tango goes in reality. You will recognize the five steps of the solution focused dance. You will also learn the context-clarifying question, the goal-setting question, and the usefulness question, three important tools of the solution-focused trade.

Mark invites the children in age order, thinking that this is the most logical approach. The first he will meet is Eric but, unexpected, Cherly shows up.

Cherly

Mark: *Hello, Cherly, good morning. Thanks for coming.*
Cherly: *Hi. I know you were expecting Eric, but he had to leave town for an*

urgent business thing. It is always the same with him, busy, busy, and busy in a kind of chaotic manner. He asked me to come in his place so here I am. Sorry that I did not let you know beforehand.

Mark: *No problem at all, Cherly. I am glad that you were so kind as to step in.*

Cherly: *Yeah, well, I step in as usual. In our family@business, I often serve as the stopgap.*

Mark lets this remark pass and continues: *Anyhow, welcome. You know that I already talked a lot with your parents about the business, the family and the family@business. In order to avoid misconceptions about you and your siblings, I would like to ask you some questions if that is OK with you.*

Cherly: *Sure. Go ahead. Oh, and thank you for asking me questions about myself because I know that there are some prejudices running around about me.*

Mark: *We all are aware that prejudices exist and we need to fight against them. That is why I always ask lots of questions. Your answers will help me to get a correct view. If I ask you a question that you deem inappropriate or that you do not want to answer, then just tell me and I will ask another question. This is not an interrogation but an interview. I want to get to know you better to see what your thoughts are and what you want for your future. I will ask similar questions to your siblings. Then I will reflect and decide what the next step forward is. This might be a meeting with the family or an additional talk with one or more persons. I will see how it goes and flows. Is that OK with you?*

Cherly: *Sure, Thanks for explaining.*

Mark: *Now, would you be so kind to tell me a little bit about yourself, how old are you, what kind of studies did you do, are you in a relationship. Personal stuff. And after that, what is your position in the family@business, what track did you already do in the company. Business stuff.*

Cherly answers all these questions and talks openly about her life. She also tells Mark that her non-executive job in the marketing department is not totally to her liking.

Cherly: *You know, Mark, I work under Alice who was employee number two in our family@business. She has always been very nice to me. She knows me since I was a child. Already in my teenage years, she was very interested in me. She feels like an aunt to me. I studied marketing but that was more of a negative choice. When I was 18, I* just did not know what I wanted to do with my life. Marketing was Alice's suggestion. Probably my father had a hand it too.

Mark: What do you mean?

Cherly: As children we did not see much of our Daddy. He was always working and travelled a lot. I think he did a great job as entrepreneur, but he could never have done it without my Mom. I still don't know how he did it but as a father, he was always there when necessary. He showed up unexpectedly when I graduated. I remember when I was a little girl, my cat was killed by a truck and I was very sad. I thought Daddy was at the factory but all of a sudden, he was there, and he stayed with me for the rest of the day. I can give you many examples. I think my brother and sister will tell you the same. Daddy: ever absent and always close. So, to answer your question: I think Daddy arranged it with Alice that she would take me under her wings.

Mark: Did you ever ask one of them?

Cherly: Alice would never tell something without consent of Daddy and Daddy just denied it. He said that marketing was a good basis for later.

Mark: Talking about later, what do we need to talk about so that our conversation will be useful to you?

Cherly: It is maybe a little pretentious, and by the way, in this family we hate pretentiousness, but I feel that I have outgrown my current position. I am so much in my comfort-zone that I am sometimes just bored, and I don't bother to show up in time like the rest of the employees. The only jobs I get, are the easiest that require no effort at all, let alone creativity. In the beginning I liked that because it was failsafe. But now I feel I gained some self-confidence and I would like to take it one step further.

Mark: That is wonderful. How did you find out?

Cherly: We had professor Hange over and she made us do that BLEEP exercise.

Mark: Excuse me, what exercise?

Cherly: It was actually called "the Boost your Leadership Exercise" but Daddy renamed it into BLEEP. At first, I was reluctant to go along because I was afraid that I would not be able to do it. I did not want to disappoint my parents and at that time I certainly did not need something that made me doubt even more about myself. So first I refused. But later I called professor Hange and I did the exercise anyway. As a matter of fact, I redid the exercise a few weeks ago.

Mark: Did you tell someone about this?

Cherly: No. My parents always overprotected me and that made me feel weak. As kid and youngster, I of course enjoyed the perks of their overprotecting, but I came to realize that it did not help me to grow *into a confident person. After I did the BLEEP thing, I had several sessions with professor Hange and that was really helpful. I paid for them myself, so this happened discretely.*

Mark: *Congratulations. Correct me if I am wrong but it seems like you are really working hard not only in your job but especially on yourself. And by doing this all by yourself, you prove to be a courageous and proactive young lady. Don't you think the time has come to be a little bit more outspoken?*

Cherly: *Maybe but I am afraid that I have my image against me. Everybody thinks I am the spoilt brat because I am the youngest. Well, I admit I am spoiled but I am no longer the brat I used to be. You want to know some ugly family stuff?*

Mark: *Only if you think it is useful so that we talk about it in such a way that you can make progress with it.*

Cherly: *Isn't that your job, Mark?*

Mark: *I like your assertiveness. And yes, that is my task.*

Cherly: *Take Eric for example. Just like today, he uses me as a stopgap whenever he needs one. I know he is very busy and that he takes a lot of load on his shoulders because he always wants to impress Daddy. I understand that and I even respect him for what he does for the company. But still, I hate it when he treats me like an intern and only trusts me with basic stuff. Whenever he is nervous, he is snappy, you will see for yourself.*

Mark: *What would you like to be different?*

Cherly: *That my family takes me seriously. If that happens, the employees will certainly follow.*

Mark: *What do you need to do to make this happen?*

Cherly: *Maybe I make it more difficult for myself than necessary. I know for a fact that I have made progress. I could start with telling this to Alice, I could tell her that I had successful sessions with professor Hange after I did the BLEEP. I could ask her to give me more challenging work and ask her to coach me instead of protecting me against failure. I am sure she will talk to Daddy about this and when it comes from her, he will talk to Mom. Then the rest of the family will know from them.*

Mark: *Then what?*

Cherly: *Then I want to create successes with the projects that Alice entrusts me with. Actions and certainly results, have more power of expression than words. If I can show results, I don't have to explain nor defend myself against this fixed image that people have of me.*

Mark: *Wow. That sounds great.*

Cherly: *I do hope that Eric will not intervene like he usually does. Whenever he did this, we always had a big fight at family gatherings. I never*

*succumbed to the temptation of starting those fights at the office.
Our parents instilled us with the taboo of never mixing private with
business and although that is easier said than done, it still is sound
advice.*

Mark: *Correct. How did those fights end?*

Cherly: *Oh, always in the same manner. Ella steps in as the go-between. We
call her the family doctor, and sometimes the family psychiatrist
since she was very little. But I admire her for that and for what she
does with her life.*

Mark: *Seems like you have a normal family! (both laugh) Now what is it
that you want us to talk about so that in the future you more often
find your own voice, get more challenging tasks and develop a
stronger image than today?*

Cherly: *I think we already covered a lot today. I will start out with talking to
Alice and brace myself for more tough jobs. Do you want to know
my deepest secret?*

Mark: *If you think that is useful for me to know, yes.*

Cherly: *Within a few years I want Alice's position in the family@business,
and I want to be more involved in strategic decision making. That
will allow me to make a real and positive difference for the company.
I still have a lot to learn so I will go slow.*

Mark: *Wow. Great plan.*

When Cherly leaves his office, Mark starts taking some notes about the
interview. Ten minutes later he gets a phone call from Cherly.

Cherly: *Can we talk?*

Mark: *Sure, go ahead.*

Cherly: *I'd like to thank you for our talk. And I realized that you are right.
I urgently need to be more active and even proactive. I particularly
like your suggestion that I should come on time, and even a little
earlier than the rest. That will show them that I am serious about my
next steps.*

Mark: *Mmm, well,… OK.*

Cherly: *Thanks. Let's talk soon.*

Mark: *Goodbye.*

Mark

Mark is astonished that Cherly put words in his mouth that he never ut-
tered. He sees this as a sign that Cherly really is intending to do something
about her position in the family@business. Mark is happy that Cherly came
up with this simple plan, visible for everybody so that it will set progress
in motion.

As you have read, Mark does not avoid problematic issues, but he also does not pursue them. He focuses on the resources that he defines as whatever the client can use to obtain his or her goals. For Cherly the resources that she showed in this conversation are her willingness to step in for her brother, the fact that she does not make fuzz about being used as a stopgap, her affection for Alice, her respect for her parents and their accomplishments. She showed courage and initiative in her work with professor Hange and has a plan for her future. Her first action has been decided – showing up in time. Engagement toward the family@business is clear and the necessary insight into herself means she knows what elements need to change for the better. She is assertive towards Mark without being aggressive.

Once you learn to look at people through the spectacles of possibilities, you will discover more and more resources.

Eric

A few days after Mark talked to Cherly, Eric calls.

Eric:	Hi. It's me. Can you come to my office tomorrow at 17h00 sharp?
Mark:	Hi Mister Eric, my name is Mark. Thank you for calling me.
Eric:	Deal?
Mark:	I will free my agenda and come over to your office.
Eric:	Thanks. (Ends call abruptly)
Mark (to himself):	Snappy indeed.

The next day, at Eric's office, 17h00 sharp

Eric: Welcome. Sorry I was so rude yesterday. I was in a hurry because I needed to get the financial statements ready for the board. And I wanted a speedy appointment with you.

Mark: OK, thanks for apologizing. Don't worry, this also happens to me sometimes. When I am stressed or worried or just tired, then I get snappy.

Eric: Oh.

Mark: When I noticed that this snappiness landed badly with my collaborators, I decided to train myself so that I stay calm and courteous. I must say that I am happy with that change. People are much more cooperative since then.

Eric: Oh. Is that a suggestion?

Mark: That is for you to decide.

Eric: Wow, you sure don't beat around the bush. That's an immediate start. I am glad that finally my parents took the initiative concerning *succession. I have been suggesting this to my Daddy since a few years but until recently he always said it was too early. I haven't insisted on the topic because I don't want to come across a greedy. I am just worried about what might happen with our family@business if nothing is settled. As siblings we might end up in limbo. It might be a very costly inheritance. Our employees and other stakeholders might get worried. Well, I want to prevent that from happening.*

Mark: *That is very reasonable of you. Yet it also shows your respectful stance that you never pushed the topic.*

Eric: *Thank you.*

Mark: *Can I ask you some questions please?*

Mark now uses the same introduction as with Cherly and asks the context-clarifying question of step 2 in the Solution Tango. Eric talks freely about his life and work and about his track until now.

When asked the goal setting question from step 3, Eric answers as follows: *The mere fact that we are having this conversation and that you as an outsider are invited by my parents to facilitate this process, is useful in itself.*

Mark: *Very good. And for you personally, what do we need to talk about so that this conversation will be useful to you?*

Eric: *My first concern is the future of the company. Since I was a child, my Dad always called me "my successor." I never knew anything other than that I would be coming into the company. For me it has always been obvious that I would become an engineer like my father. I do realize that our company has grown big and that it is no longer a one-man show. Plus, I have two sisters that eventually will become co-owners. So, we will have to think and talk how we will do this together.*

Mark: *You are absolutely right. it seems like you give priority to the company, over your personal ambitions. That shows that your loyalty to what we family@business consultants often call, "the eldest child in the family."*

Eric: *I have read some books; I even was in seminars about succession in family@business. But I realize that theoretical knowledge will not solve the puzzle.*

Mark: *Puzzle?*

Eric: *Yes, puzzle. The family puzzle plus our top management puzzle.*

Mark: *Please explain.*

Eric: *Our family is not used to talking about delicate topics. We are do-ers and not talkers. Plus, we too often operate in the mode: what you can do by yourself is both quicker and better. Concerning the future of our family@business, we will have to talk about delicate issues.*

Mark: *Can you give me an example?*

Eric: Well, you have talked to my parents and to my youngest sister, so you should already have an idea about this.

Mark: Yes, but I do not want to risk hasty conclusions and being trapped in my own analysis that might be wrong or at least incomplete. So please expand.

Eric: it is no secret that I do not have the best of relationships with my youngest sister Cherly. This started during that situation with her fiancé Jeff, luckily by now ex-fiancé. Another delicate topic is the question of money. I know for a fact that my parents are rich but they keep talking as if they are destitute, as if the company is going broke every two months. Every time we discuss finance with our accountant and financial director, Dad is constantly "yes-but-ting." Yes, but the economy is in a slump, Yes, but sales prices are going down and our margins are shrinking. Yes, but our competitors are becoming stronger every day. Yes, but what will happen if we lose our customers. Etcetera. It drives our financial experts, and me crazy. If we try to talk sense into him, Mom jumps on the wagon and says that we have not been there at the beginning of the company, how difficult it was, how they have been through hard times, that we see things too lightly, etcetera.

Mark: Maybe they are just....

Eric: Worried, yes, I know, everybody says so. But still it is not very productive. Well, I think we will have to try and live with it.

Mark: Maybe that is for the best.

Eric: You know the story of Cherly and her ex-fiancé?

Mark: No. Will it be helpful if you tell me about it?

Eric: Maybe, I don't know. Jeff is the son of Bert, the first employee that my parents ever hired. Bert was Dad's best friend in those days. As the business grew from a small software start-up to a general contractor and real estate firm, Bert was always on board. First as a programmer, later as manager of the growing teams of technicians and in the last phase, he was Vice President Operations. Well, that was one promotion too much. He started making big and costly mistakes. Mind you, Bert has always been very closely involved with the company and my parents saw him as part of the family. When I first came to work here after finishing my studies, I did a big round of all the companies and subsidiaries to get to learn the company from the inside out. I went around for months asking questions about whatever came to my mind. Since all employees knew me they were very open and welcoming. I learned a great deal. But I also discovered mistakes, wrong decisions with negative consequences for the company and –worst of all– a lot of cover-ups in the areas where Bert had the final responsibility. Because Bert knows me since I was born, I was a bit intimidated to talk about this. One day I was on a *business trip abroad together with Bert and I decided to ask him about some of these issues. Bert was first irritated and when I kept asking questions, he became enraged. In his anger he started yelling at me: "how dare you, snot-nosed little brat, to doubt me. I have been doing this job since before you learned to read and write. Now don't you dare to talk about this to your Daddy!" I knew enough then, took the next plane home and prepared a file on the mistakes and cover-ups that I discovered. After that I went to Dad's office. He would not believe me in the beginning, but he studied my files. That was a tough week for my parents because they realized that something had to be done with this. Dad asked me to interview some middle managers in a discreet manner. Almost all of the elder employees were appreciative of Bert but the younger ones not so. One of them asked me if he could be blunt. I of course said yes. He told me: "Bert is the Peter's principle in the flesh. A very nice person but since he became VP Operations, he no longer can cope with the high level of that job." After I shared all the information with my parents, Dad procrastinated for a few weeks. I could tell how sad both of my parents were that they at least had to demote their good friend and ally from the beginning. The week after that, he invited me for a meeting with the company's lawyer. We created a very generous severance package for Bert. My father had a meeting with Bert in our family home, the content of which I have never learned. Since it was the 25th anniversary of the company, we had a big party some weeks later. At that party, our parents gave big speeches. They also announced that Bert had decided to take an early pension and gave him a big farewell present. It was probably the most elegant way to solve this unfortunate incident. Everybody happy, well, at least on first sight.*

Mark: *Remarkable story. This alas happens in family@businessses where employees can become a kind of non-family family. Combine that with the evolution towards a large and complex firm and it happens that collaborators, who were a perfect fit when the company was small, do not evolve along. I must congratulate you with your intervention. That proves that you have leadership skills and that, even when recently in the company, you found the courage to persevere. The way you prepared the file for your father shows that you worked meticulously in this delicate situation.*

Eric: *Thank you.*

Mark: *The way your parents combined the 25th anniversary of the company with a respectful goodbye to Bert shows family@business diplomacy and respect. That sent an important sign to the rest of the employees.*

Eric: *Correct, I got that feedback afterwards although some managers were happy to be rid of Bert.*

Mark: *Sure, that created free space for others to move up or in. (both laugh)*
Eric: *There was a little backfire, however.*
Mark: *Oh?*
Eric: *At that time Cherly was in a relation with Jeff who happens to be Bert's son. Jeff was furious. Right after Dad spoke to Bert, Jeff showed up at our traditional Saturday evening dinner and started yelling at my parents. I spare you the content of his words, but it was not very agreeable. Daddy showed him the door, but Jeff demanded that Cherly go with him. Which she did. She stayed away for a week and did not show up at work. Then my mother texted her that she should come back to work within two days or she would be fired. Cherly came back to work, she even moved back into her childhood room. You can imagine the tension at the office and in the house. Luckily, Ella, our family psychiatrist as we call her since she was young, intervened. She mediated between Cherly and our parents so that after a few weeks, things returned to normal; well, as normal as possible under those circumstances.*
Mark: *Phew, intense weeks that must have been.*
Eric: *Indeed. But in the end, all came around. Jeff kept pushing Cherly to side with him and his family. he pushed her too hard and Cherly broke up with him. The rest of the family had a deep sigh of relief.*
Mark: *Yeah, I can understand that. You know, what you just described to me reminds me of an important concept that is useful when thinking about families, individuals but also family@businessses: The concept of resilience.*
Eric: *Meaning?*
Mark: *Resilience is the skill to undergo life-changing events that can't be avoided because they belong to life. We are all born and we all die, to give the most obvious examples.*
Eric: *I prefer to ignore the part of dying. (Both laugh)*
Mark: *Yet we all die, preferably later than sooner. Anyhow, resilience is the skill to withstand adversity, to rebound from this adversity and to learn from this event so that when the next life-changing event takes place, it will be a little easier to tackle it.*
Eric: *Interesting concept.*
Mark: *From the examples you gave me, it shows clearly that your family members possess a healthy level of resilience. Although obviously those life changing events are painful, with this concept in mind you can always ask yourself: "what do I learn from this?"*
Eric: *Interesting I will certainly keep this in mind. Can I come back to your first question, your what I believe you call the "goal setting question."*
Mark: *Oh, you read my books?*
Eric: *Sure. When something major comes up, I always prepare myself.*
Mark: *Sure, Eric, so what do you need to talk about today so that...*

Eric: *I know the question, thank you. Like I told you, we are a warm loving family, but we are not used to talk about delicate issues. I think I sketched the nature of our family enough by now. I hope you will facilitate these conversations and steer them in the necessary directions.*

Mark: *If everybody will cooperate like you do today, that will for sure happen*

Eric: *And then we go through the usual topics like family charter, management succession where we will have to take our non-family management into account but also the role of the siblings now and in the future. There is one topic that for me is very important, namely the in-laws. For the moment, I am the only one who is married, but surely Ella and Cherly will follow in due time. It is maybe a little paranoid, but I wonder how we can prevent that an eventual divorce becomes a threat to the family@business. We all know the divorce statistics. I mention this because when I was about 16 years old, my father had a love affair. Our parents were open about that, maybe a little too open. I would have preferred not to know their private stuff. And by open, I mean fights, big fights. This never happened in the office, only at home. I remember Daddy even went to live elsewhere for a few weeks. There was open discussion and even threats from my mother about what would happen with the company if they would divorce. They had no premarital agreements so they both were full 50% owners. I think they went to see a marital therapist. That was successful. Daddy found out he was in a midlife crisis; you know stuff that happens halfway through your life and certainly after two decades of working like a madman. As children we were relieved to see and feel their love for each other grow back to where it was when we were little. They even organized a second wedding party, of course without ever telling anyone outside of our family why.*

Mark: *It seems like your family is big on parties whenever real significant events are happening.*

Eric: *Yes. When I married Lars, we made sure to make a prenuptial agreement. Because Lars also comes from an entrepreneurial family, we both realize that we have to protect the family@business against the vicissitudes of life. Like they say: a good contract is a contract written in order never to be used.*

Mark: *Wise decision.*

Eric: *I fully realize that one can never force other people to do likewise but I still think it is a topic that needs to be discussed in the family. We will of course not refer to our parent's painful period.*

Mark: *No, I don't see the use for that. Still, your topic is important, and I will see when it is an appropriate time for inserting it in the discussions. Do you have other topics that you would like us to talk about today?*

Eric: No, this is more than enough, thank you.
Mark: Was this conversation useful to you, Eric?
Eric: Sure.
Mark: What was it precisely that was useful to you?
Eric: We have touched on several important topics; we laid the ground for our upcoming work and I was able to share some of my concerns.
Mark: Great. What else?
Eric: It feels good to be able to talk about these things and know that there is discretion and confidence.
Mark: Thank you. What else?
Eric: I don't know...erm... let me think ...erm...well, maybe the way you started this conversation. I appreciate your respectful reprimand. My snappiness is indeed a point I need to work on. Thank you.
Mark: Thank you for your cooperation and openness. We will meet again soon.

Ella

Mark WhatsApps Ella because he knows she is working in a hospital and will not pick up her cell phone. She is quick to call and set a date for meeting each other the next weekend. Ella has to travel home and prefers to meet in Mark's office.

Mark: Welcome, miss Ella.
Ella: Oh, please just call me Ella.
Mark: Same here, just Mark will do. How was your week in the hospital?
Ella: Busy as usual. But it is very exciting work. I learn something new every day.

After some chitchat about her work, the inconvenience of constantly having to move every few months plus the strain that puts on her relationship, Mark asks her the goal-setting question.

Ella: You know I am exactly the same age as the company. we both have been conceived around the same time, but we are no twins.
Mark: Indeed, your 25th anniversary was...
Ella: I can assure you that the 25th anniversary party for the family@ business was a much bigger affair than my party. Actually, I think that is normal. The company is central to the lives of so many people, especially my parents. You probably heard about the retirement of Bert; our employee number 1? My Dad's speech was so respectful, even affectionate that it touched the heart of everybody who was there. I could feel his sadness that this had to happen. Still, the welfare of the company is of paramount importance to my father and

my mother. And my siblings and me feel the same. It is as if the company is the eldest child in the family. I know for sure that all employees, certainly those who have been here for some years and have witnessed the periods of growth, feel the same. It is almost like my parents created a clan.

Mark: *That is one of the beauties of a family@business.*

Ella: *Well, it also has its ugly sides. Ugly maybe is too harsh a word, downside is maybe a more appropriate term.*

Mark: *Mm.*

Ella: *What happened between Cherly and Jeff after Bert took his retirement that in actual fact was a platinum parachute out was a "downside."*

Mark: *Mm.*

Ella: *Jeff came to our house one Saturday evening, yelling and cursing, threatening my Dad, telling he would do everything possible to take revenge. The worst was that he was able to convince Cherly to leave with him. Cherly stayed away for a week. As always, I was the family mediator. I have done that since I was a kid. Mediating in the fights between Eric and Cherly, fights about the most stupid things. You know about the period our parents were on the verge of divorce.*

Mark: *I have heard about it but if it is useful to you, you can tell me your version.*

Ella: *No, I was too young and by the way, they solved it in the best possible manner. After that period, I remember it was as if their relationship and the whole of our family was renewed.*

Mark: *Perfect. To me it seems like you are not only a very clever young lady who knows exactly what she wants for her life, you have chosen an ambitious career path. You are also very connected to your family. To me, but please do correct me if I am wrong, it seems that you are both very involved in the family as well as able to take your distance and look at what happens from a meta-point of view.*

Ella: *You are correct. That is why I like being a doctor. One must both be involved with the emotions and life-happenings of the patient as well as being sufficiently detached when you need to make decisions. I recognize myself in your analysis.*

Mark: *How do you see the future for the family@business?*

Ella: *Eric will take over from Dad and that will take some time and effort. Dad is not likely to let go easily and Eric, however intelligent and hardworking he is, still is too insecure about himself. In those moments he gets snappy.*

Mark: *I have witnessed that from the front seat. (Both laugh)*

Ella: *Eric means no harm; it is just a bad habit. But when he wants to take the top leadership role, he will have to work on that, don't you think so?*

Mark: *Mm.*

Ella: *I told him so and he just grumbled but I think he realizes that it is true. For myself, I see no executive nor operational role in the family@business. Unless I sell the shares that will come to me, I will be just a shareholder. But I'd like to be on the Board.*

Mark: *How do you see your role there?*

Ella: *First I want to know what is happening and second I will be able to mediate whenever conflicts arise. And believe me, they will. Plus, I want to stay involved with the company, albeit from a certain distance.*

Mark: *Sound plan.*

Ella: *The only thing that worries me for the future cooperation, as family is Cherly's position. She and Eric have always been antagonistic. He thinks that Cherly is a spoiled brat. She thinks that Eric is too full of himself. It is not that they fight all the time. No, they are respectful. But there is a big distance between them.*

Mark: *Oh.*

Ella: *On top of that, I think Cherly is not too happy with her current job. She told me so. I try to encourage her to do an additional study so that she builds both her self-confidence and her image in the family and amongst the employees. I do hope she will do this.*

Mark: *Although you are in the midst of building your own career and very busy, you are very supportive towards your siblings. From what you tell me, I can imagine that everybody appreciates your contributions.*

Ella: *Thanks, but for me this is normal, that is who I am.*

Mark: *Do you think in the upcoming months you can spare time to be involved with the meetings, discussion and conversations that we will need to have in order to tackle the family@business management and ownership succession?*

Ella: *Sure, this is a priority. I hope I don't need to be here too much. Do you work in the weekends?*

Mark: *Sure. I do that all the time. During the week, the business must go on. However important this process is for family and business, still the business –like the show–must go on.*

Ella: *So, what is the next step now?*

Mark tells Ella that he will take some time to reflect and then he will have a meeting with the parents. After that, he will schedule a family meeting to open the conversations up around all the different topics necessary for the future.

Conclusion

You saw how to use the genogram, learned about systemic thinking and the five-step tango of the solution-focused interview, but you also had a glimpse of how reality unfolds in a real family and a real family@business.

We touched upon themes that occur frequently but are seldom discussed: nonfamily family, demoting or even firing someone who has been closely involved in the history of the family@business, strife between siblings, life cycle drama's like the near-collapse of John and Annie's marriage, family@ business group dynamics, etc.

The Next Gen now is ready for tools that will help them take their next step.

Note

1 McGoldrick M. and Gerson R. 2020 Genograms: Assessment and Intervention, WW Norton & Co, 2020. This is the fourth edition of the classic handbook on the topic.

Chapter 11

Next Gen: Eight Tools for Your Future

Generic Tools

Everybody who is in the same predicament as the John and Annie family can use the tools that we present here. If you, the Reader is working in a family@business, you can use these tools to assess yourself and create a self-development plan in which you monitor your progress.

Furthermore, these tools – just like all the insights in this book – can be used to design Next Gen workshops, retreats, and mentoring programs. The tools come in handy for professionals offering services to their family@business clients.

Obviously, the professionals can use the tools under to hone their own skills. Plus, these tools also serve managers in non-family businesses. In short, they are universally applicable.

The Siblings

We are now in late phase three in the Family@business Life cycle (see Chapter 2). The parents are in their fifties and the children are in their twenties. They enjoyed their education, went to their respective schools, and grew into young adults. Eric and Cherly already work in the family@business and Ella is in medical school. Their parents took the courage to start thinking and discussing about their future plans. They involved family@business specialists to coach them, their children, and their employees through this stressful event that is called succession in which they have no experience whatsoever.

The First John and Annie Family Meeting

Mark organizes a meeting with the family. John and Annie declined to participate with the argument: "It is their first time together; we do want them to speak freely and openly. There will be enough meetings with all of us later on."

DOI: 10.4324/9781003194200-11

After welcoming everybody, Prof. Hange gives a little seminar on the eight tools.

Cynthia: *Welcome. Mark and myself are happy that we are invited to help you take the next steps. In recent months we worked on the leadership indicators and you did the "Boost your Leadership Potential Exercise" which, if I understand correctly, within your family is nicknamed the BLEEP exercise. (all smile). Mark worked with you on the four challenges: morphing from child into employee, respect, trust and sibling relationships. Two weeks ago, I mailed you an article on the eight tools that you can use to prepare your future role in or outside the family@business. I do hope that you took some time to read it and reflect upon it.*

Mark: *Cynthia will give you a synopsis of the article so that all minds are primed in the same direction. After that we will answer whatever questions you have and then we will invite you to do an exercise for yourself. After that exercise, we will open the discussion amongst you.*

Cynthia: *Maybe you will work together in the company or maybe not. Most probably, Ella will take no active job in the company. Both Cherly's and Eric's job will change, evolve and grow over the coming years. Whatever happens, one certainty remains: you are siblings so there is no escape from co-operating for the simple reason that one day you will become co-owners.*

Mark: *Some of you will use all of the tools, some will use only a few, some of you will choose which tools to begin with. Choose what fits best with who you are at this moment. Of course, your specific situation also is important, but leadership always starts from the inside out. Time, effort and experience will help you mastering your basic self-leadership skills. With personal leadership mastery comes greater proficiency in situational leadership.*

Cynthia: *Having said all this, let us look at the eight tools.*

Eight Tools to Help the Next Gen Prepare For the Future

1. Lust for Learning

    Before your 12th year, your parents mostly drive your education. But after your 12th year – in most countries around the world and particularly your socio-economic circles – choices open up. As already discussed, learning is more important than knowledge. And learning-to-learn tops even that. So, it is less important what you study. It is more important how you study. And it is of utter importance that you study hard.

The broader your basic education, the larger the platform from which your education can expand in all possible directions. We know a successful multinational entertainment company that was founded by someone with an M.A. in philosophy.

In this ever faster-changing world of disruption, be prepared to enjoy a life of learning by cultivating your curiosity for and wonderment at things novel.

2. Look outside

Look outside yourself and look out to the big physical and intellectual world out there. And the outside world certainly is bigger than your family@business cocoon. Creating as many connections as possible will enlarge your learning network and create a robust "University of Life" for you.

Tools to do this are travel, business school and charity networks, clubs, sports, culture events, books, etc.

The only thing you need to do is: reach out.

3. Self-awareness

Be self-conscious and aware of your own behavior. When little children are playing, they forget that there is a difference between play and reality, between "as if" and "such is." Growing up requires a growing awareness that there is a reality out there of which we are part but which at the same time is separate from us. Gradually we can and need to learn that reality has an impact on us and that we have an impact on our surrounding reality. In puberty we might see the world only from the inside out: I am central in my life. Adolescence brings the notion that we are part of social circles. In these developmental years, we become self-conscious and learn how our being and acting has impact on and is impacted by what happens around us. How we are able to deal with this, is a precursor of how we will deal with other people in the future.

4. Self-confidence

Self-confidence is not a black-white phenomenon but rather a continuum between low and high. So, in order to train your self-confidence, you have to start – as a youngster – with rather some easy tasks where failure is not probable and then work yourself towards more and more difficult tasks. When you are a small child, your parents and teachers will help you setting these tasks that with age become more difficult. When your benevolent caretakers notice you become expedient in a task, they will raise the bar slightly. That you can learn to work for your successes, and it will build your self-confidence. Slowly as you grow older and more mature, you can take things into your own hands by setting yourself ever more difficult goals. You can do this in your studies but also in sports, music, debating clubs, ... wherever you feel it is useful for making progress. The old saying can be a guiding rule: 'Plus Est En Vous' (More is in You).

5. Move beyond your comfort zone

When you are in your comfort zone, you are at ease: things feel familiar and in control. Low levels of stress and anxiety permit you to perform on a steady level. There is a 'business as usual' air. But you don't learn to stretch your skills so there is little or no advancement. Stepping out of your comfort zone raises anxiety and generates a stress response. This results in an enhanced level of concentration and focus. The art is to develop a feeling for the correct balance: too much comfort zone and nothing new is learned, too far out of your comfort zone and you enter a "danger zone" in which your performance rapidly declines under the influence of greater anxiety. Balance is key.

6. Adopt resilience and adapt to change

You remember the concept of resilience we introduced in Chapter 4. In brief: resilience is the skill to undergo difficult situations, find a way out and learn from this process. For a youngster, difficult situations can be anything: bad results in school, family disputes over pocket money, fights over how late one must be back from a party, losing the first boy/girlfriend, etc. These are all moments when your resilience is challenged and if it turns out right, your skill at resilience grows. Basically, this means that you learn to undergo and to rebound from these unhappy or even painful experiences.

Through these experiences, you will learn to accept that your life's path is strewn with unavoidable difficulties and problems. Using Formula-P you have learned to recreate your problems into challenges. Instead of an anxious problem-avoider, you turn yourself into an agile solution builder.

7. Be sensitive to long-term strategy

Of course, you have to do the daily work, but that is not enough for Next Gen entrepreneurs. A passion for strategy that includes a long-term vision is one of the indicators of Leadership Potential, as you learned in Chapter 4. Like a sailor, you need to make sure you don't crash on the next wave and at the same time keep an eye on the horizon and weather forecast for the next day. You can't look into the future, but you need to constantly focus your attention on it.

8. Communication skills

Sharing what you think and feel about issues in (non) verbal language and through your actions is in essence done by communication. Communication consists of two equally important parts: sending and receiving information. In plain English: talking and listening. The task of a leader is to create impact on others and this is only possible when you master the skill of effective communication.

> The action is in the interaction: what happens between people's noses is even more important than what happens between their ears.

The John and Annie Family Meeting, Continued

Cherly: *WOW, that's interesting. Your explanation makes the article so much more alive. Thank you.*

Eric: *Indeed. There are so many elements in these tools that are useful.*

Ella: *These tools seem to me to be as useful to a doctor as to a businessperson. But knowing them is one; making use of them is another.*

Mark: *Here we can help you. We designed exercises so that you can apply the tools and see how they work for each of you.*

All: *great, let's do this.*

The Use of Scaling Questions

Mark presents the different forms. Basically, it is an exercise in self-awareness and self-monitoring. To avoid black-white positions, Mark offers a scaling question for each tool. One is asked to consider each of the tools above and then use the form that goes with the tool. The process is very alike for each tool:

- The zero position means: this tool is totally absent in me
- The 10 position means: this tool is perfect for me
- Start with where you are now, give it a number on a scale from 0 to 10
- Write down details about your current position.
- What would be the smallest next step? If you, e.g. position yourself on number 3, what is in that number and what would you do/think/feel different when you will be on a 4.
- What do you need in order to be able to make this little step forward? What else?

You can do this for every tool. You can do this exercise on your own and discuss the details with each other.

Watch out! The given numbers are NOT measuring points on a mathematical scale. Then the scale question would turn into an exam and lose its versatility. The points on the scale are only metaphors for difference.

The form looks like this:

Next Gen Preparations

	Abscent									Perfect
Tool 1	1	2	3	4	5	6	7	8	9	10

Describe details:

Next Step Requirements:

Tool 2	1	2	3	4	5	6	7	8	9	10

Describe details:

Next Step Requirements:

Tool 3	1	2	3	4	5	6	7	8	9	10

Describe details:

Next Step Requirements:

Tool 4	1	2	3	4	5	6	7	8	9	10

Describe details:

Next Step Requirements:

Tool 5	1	2	3	4	5	6	7	8	9	10

Describe details:

Next Step Requirements:

Tool 6	1	2	3	4	5	6	7	8	9	10

Describe details:

Next Step Requirements:

Tool 7	1	2	3	4	5	6	7	8	9	10

Describe details:

Next Step Requirements:

Tool 8	1	2	3	4	5	6	7	8	9	10

Describe details:

Next Step Requirements:

Mark: *Or you can look at each tool in a slightly different manner without using numbers. This avoids the misunderstanding that this scaling exercise is a measurement tool while in essence it is a tool to help people get the best possible sense of nuances. To make that clearer and to help you design similar tools for different situations, let us give you an example we call: the "Move beyond your comfort zone"-tool. You can just reflect about the answers, but it is much more effective to also take notes. You can do likewise for all the other tools.*

Exercise for tool 5: Stretch-your-comfort-zone:

- Discover your comfort zone: what situations and topics you are full at ease with? Consider this your baseline.
- In which situations do you feel stressed and anxious and are you ill at ease
- Visualize both positions on a continuum, like black and white.
- Where are you now?
- What is the smallest step out of your comfort zone?
- Describe this and experiment with it.
- How does this feel and what is your performance? Feels ok? Take the next step forward.
- Does not feel OK and the results are bad? Take one step back.

Q&A

Mark: *Do you have questions, remarks or suggestions?*

Eric: *Yes, I suggest that we do the exercises at home so that we can take the time that each of us finds necessary and useful.*

Mark: *If all the others feel the same, that is fine with us. Other questions.*

Ella: *Is the sequence of the eight tools important?*

Mark: *Good question. As a matter of fact, the sequence is not important. We suggest even that you put the eight tools in the sequence that fits best with your needs. Maybe you find some of the tools irrelevant for yourself. Or maybe you think of other tools that would fit your needs better. We offer you these eight tools because they have proven to be useful for most people in your situation.*

Cynthia: *Please keep in mind that these tools are what the name tells you they are: tools. They are not Nobel-Prize winning truths. (All laugh)*

Mark:	*Indeed. All that these tools offer you are working hypotheses. If they fit your advancement, make use of them. If your find other tools that are more useful to you, feel free. But of course, the tools we present you have been thoroughly thought through and are well documented in the professional literature[1] in our field.*
Cynthia:	*And please do not make the mistake of answering in a socially desirable manner or treat the number and their content as if this is an exam. The scaling questions we offer you or, if, you prefer the visualizations, are tools to help you think about yourself in a differentiated mode.*
Mark:	*The nice thing in this exercise is that you document your efforts so that you can monitor your progress over the coming months. That will help you chart your progress.*
Cherly:	*Thanks for explaining and especially thanks for giving us these nuances. A misunderstanding is easily made. Now, speaking for myself, I also prefer to prepare on my own and then have a coaching session with you, Mark or Cynthia so that you can help me speed up my learning process.*
Mark:	*Cynthia and myself are happy to be of your assistance.*
Eric:	*I don't think I need that help, I can cope on my own.*
Cherly:	*Typical Eric. Why don't you learn to be a little bit more open about yourself? It won't hurt you.*
Eric:	*Yeah, typical Cherly, the I-know-better.*
Ella:	*Don't start your classical arguments please. You should really learn to tackle your differences in other manners. I know you are not so different. Your continuous arguing and bickering are just old but bad habits.*
Eric (talking to Mark and Cynthia):	*See. What did I tell you? Ella, the eternal go-between.*
Cynthia:	*Anyhow, good that you are so open, even with us, outsiders in the room. Giving what you just showed us, this might be the right time to talk about effective communication, don't you agree.*
All:	*Go ahead.*
Cynthia:	*Let me give you a list of the seven best practices of effective communication. Mind you, they are easy to understand, but not easy to use. When things get difficult, emotions often take over and these rules of communication are thrown out. So, practicing these rules is necessary.*

Seven Best Practices for effective communication:

1   Don't beat around the bush
2   Use simple language
3   Ask for feedback after delivering a message
4   Listening is your most important asset
5   Smart people are able to explain complicated things in simple language
6   Never underestimate the power of silence
7   Communication co-creates a new reality

Cynthia:	*Think about which of those practices you are good at and in which of them, you could need some additional training.*
Mark:	*Let's make it even more interesting. Let's again use a scaling for each characteristic, put yourself on a scale from zero, equaling "I lack this totally," till 10 which stands for 'I am totally perfect in this."*
All:	*Makes sense.*
Mark:	*And to make it even more exciting and challenging, give each other a number on the same scales.*
Cherly:	*You are asking for an open fight!*
Eric:	*For once I agree with Cherly. Scaling each other's practices will lead to nothing but trouble.*
Ella:	*Not if you take this exercise seriously and instead of hitting each other over the head with really low numbers just for the sake of giving each other bad press, why don't we start interacting differently, more respectfully and certainly more effectively? After all, whether you like it or not, we're stuck together like Cynthia told us in the beginning of this meeting.*
Eric to Cherly:	*Ok, Sis, let's give it a try, OK?*
Cherly to Eric:	*OK, Big Brother, let's go. I really want to be able to work on our relationship and deep in my heart I know you want the same.*
Mark:	*Don't forget that this exercise is a tool to help you hone your communication skills. It is – and I stress this – not a school exam to see who does worst or best!*
Cynthia:	*How long a time do you think is useful before we meet again to discuss and learn from this exercise?*
Eric:	*We are all very busy but, and I quote your number one best practice, let's not beat around the bush, let's meet again fairly quickly. What do you think, Sisters?*
Cherly and Ella:	*Perfect. Two weeks?*
Mark:	*Great, let's set the date for sharing your work on both the Next Gen preparation tools and the communication skills.*

The Solution Focused Consultants do a Postmortem

Mark: That went OK, I think.

Cynthia: Sure. I am happy that they showed us their normal behavior. It is always so much more difficult when clients show us a sanitized interaction. Their openness is a sign that the quality of their family relationship is good. As we have seen in Chapter 1, this is the single most important predictor for successful succession.

Mark: I agree. And they don't talk like out of a textbook on family businesses. (both laugh) They are just normal human beings and not cardboard figures.

Cynthia: We will help them make steps forward in the next meeting so that they can make progress on the eight tools and on the seven best practices for effective communication.

Mark: But even more important for their future and their cooperation in the family@business, is that they make progress in their interaction by accepting and discussing their similarities and differences in these tools and practices. After that step, we probably need to get their parents involved and have meetings with the family as a whole in order to discuss the possible future scenarios for the family@ business.

Cynthia: I don't know how your experience is, Mark, but I prefer to present the myriad of possible future scenarios to the Founders-Owners first, without the children being present. That gives them the broadest scope of possibilities.

Mark: I always do the same. After all, the family@business still is their property and they should feel free to do with it what they deem fit to do with it, without being hampered by "We should and we ought to." All too often the G1 parents have tunnel vision in which they feel obliged to hand the business over to the children.

Cynthia: Just like too often the G2 offspring have tunnel vision in which they feel obliged to step into the family@business.

Mark: By the way, after we work through all possible scenario's (Chapter 11), we will show the Next Gen what they can do before and after their final commitment to step into the family@ business (Chapter 13).

Cynthia: When they are ready with these steps, we will offer them tools to handle the relationships with their stakeholders, the Three Circle Model (Chapters 14).

Mark: Yes, and we will top this off with family@business strategy instruments. Collective Ambition, Family Charter and the straightforward business Strategy will complete their toolbox (Chapters 16 and 17).

Cynthia: *All of this will take some time obviously but it will help the family and the business to become future-proof. Well, as future-proof as possible.*

Conclusion

All family@businessses have a broad scope of possible options when they have to decide about their future. We will explain those options in the next chapter.

Note

1 By the way, Dear Reader, everything we offer you in this book are best practices that stem from experience and research (see bibliography)

Chapter 12

Generational Transfer, Sale, or IPO?

Next Gen Scenarios

Worldwide the baby boom generation (born between 1945 and 1964) is on the verge of retirement. This means that thousands upon thousands of family businesses are confronted with a generational transition.

Every individual is unique, every family is unique and therefore every Family Business is unique. This implies that the way a Family Business transitions to the next generation also is unique. Although there are no ready-made or one-size-fits-all solutions, there are a lot of possible scenarios. There is a myriad of combinatorial possibilities, but no mathematics exists that can show you what the best choice is.

John and Annie

After the meetings with the siblings, Mark had a talk with John and Annie in which he summarized his conversations with their children.

Mark: *Before we go further, as a professional family@business advisor, I must remind you of the fact that there are also several other options concerning the future of your company.*

John: *What do you mean, Mark?*

Mark: *All too often I notice that within family@businesses, clients tend to focus exclusively on succession within the family. Mind you, I notice the same in the world of family@business advisors and researchers that sometimes treat succession within the family as something sacred. In my opinion, this is too limiting and can lead to severe problems.*

Annie: *It is only natural that one looks into your own family. Nobody with children is immune to the "my kid, nice kid"-syndrome. Look at us, after one meeting, what do I say, even before meeting you, Mark, somewhere deep in our hearts it was kind of obvious that the children would take over from us.*

DOI: 10.4324/9781003194200-12

John: *I agree even if I never thought of this. But you are right, Mark. So, tell us about the other options.*
Mark: *Great, I have to congratulate you with your open mind. Like Frank Zappa said: the mind is like a parachute, it only functions when open.*
John: *Frank who? Is that another of your colleagues?*
Mark: *Never mind, John. Let me tell you about other possibilities, or actually, they are more like possible scenarios.*

Scenario 1: Do Nothing

Unfortunately, the most common scenario is that nothing is done and that things can go their own way. Even if common sense dictates that this option leads to a final and inescapable catastrophe, this option is the most common, certainly when the founder-owner still is relatively young (40–55 years).

Even if this option is totally irrational, why is it that those younger entrepreneurs tend to stay stuck in the "after me the Flood" option?

Some classical arguments are:

1   we do not know (or want others) to know what the company is worth because it might result in unwanted reactions;
2   the legal and fiscal situation in our country is not stable
3   we do not know how to finance the takeover.

In this day and age, there are perfect solutions for all these arguments, which can simply be bought from experts.

The real reason why so many founders-owners are reluctant to think about and act upon their succession is of an emotional and psychological nature.

The issue of succession confronts the founder-owner with his own mortality, which is a topic most people tend to avoid. How come? Generation One entrepreneurs often fear that succession amounts to a loss of identity and fear that retirement will drag them into a black void. It happens that both parents are afraid that disputes among the children might pop up when talking about all the consequences of succession. All too often there is a taboo on discussing financial matters. Parents are afraid that openly discussing their financial status might 'spoil' the kids while the children fear that talking about money might make them look greedy.

You can be confronted with the **DADD syndrome** after which you no longer have the final control over your succession. DADD stands for **D**eath, **A**ccident, **D**isease, and **D**ivorce. When you do nothing proactive and wait until DADD hits, you, your family, and your business are likely to get stuck in a financial and legal quagmire. Prevention, as always is the best medicine against this dreadful crisis that might hurt or even kill your life's work.

For all these reasons, open communication and careful planning of the succession is the only safe solution.

John and Annie

John:	*I know of someone like that, Freddy, he is a member of my country club, 78 years old, tough as a whip, sharp as a knife. He always boasts that a company needs one chief and that is him. He is a very successful brewer, owner of a family@business in the third generation. His only son is 56 and is only allowed to do executive work.*
Annie:	*Yes, Freddy seems like he has eternal life. The stamina of this fellow! He beats everybody on the tennis court.*
Mark:	*I hope he has some contingency plans for when the inevitable will happen.*
John:	*Knowing Freddy, I am pretty certain he has foreseen everything. He is the kind of guy that can startle everybody, his son, his management and his clients included, with decisions that only will be made public the day after his funeral.*
Annie:	*That definitely is not how we are going to do it.*
Mark:	*Life can be harsh in unexpected and unforeseen ways. Are you familiar with the expression DADD?*
Annie:	*Never heard of.*
Mark:	*DADD stands for Death, Accident, Disease, and Divorce. All of these can be dangerous for person, family, and business.*
Annie:	*Oh, well, if that is the meaning of DADD, we are familiar with it, don't we, Daddy.*
John (blushing):	*Do we have to talk about that? Please not again.*
Mark:	*Do you think it is useful that we talk about it?*
John:	*I don't think so but I know that Annie sees this differently.*
Annie:	*I sure do! Sooner or later it will pop up anyhow. By the way, who of the children talked about this? Eric probably, didn't he?*
Mark:	*mmm, well, mmm…*
Annie:	*Yeah, yeah, professional confidentiality I presume. Never mind, Mark, I know my children.*
Mark:	*I don't doubt that at all. And, mmm, thank you.*
Annie:	*Sometimes, a client has to rescue a consultant (laughs). Sorry, John, but for me, it is important that we talk about this DADD's thing. As a couple, we survived your affair, as a person I survived my breast cancer. Although those*

were hard, really hard times, we got through them. I am
not saying that what doesn't kill you makes you stronger,
because that would feel cynical to me. I do say that we got
through that period, relatively unscathed. And most
important, our kids nor the company suffered too much.

John (to Mark): See, Mark, what a strong woman my Annie is. She is the
best thing that happened in my life.

Annie: However difficult, I am a strong believer in
communication. Silencing these grave matters is
definitely not how we are going to do this. Now it is off
my chest and that feels good. Besides, the children are all
well aware of what happened just like they are well aware
that we became stronger and ever more united after this
period. I do hope that none of them will ever have to live
through their own DADD but they are prepared.

Mark: Now I even understand better why all of your children are
so proud of their parents. To discuss further possible
scenarios would it be OK if I make a drawing?

Mark draws the following schedule on a flowchart:

Mark explains: This schedule actually is a continuum without fixed points. One extreme is when one chooses to do nothing at all and the other extreme is when one decides to sell the company as a whole. Right in the middle, you find the succession within the family and even that scenario can have many possible nuances, of which later more. Between doing nothing and intra-family succession, lies the scenario where an external and/or non-family family member, a manager with long-standing trust within the family, or a specially chosen professional takes an interregnum and acts – temporarily – as an intermediate pope. Between intra-family succession and selling the company, you can find the scenario where non-family professionals – often managers that have been in the company for a long time and have earned the trust of the family or total outsiders – buy-in into the ownership via a management buy-in/out. In the case of a very large family business, listing the company on the stock exchange via IPO can be a method to capitalize on the ownership. In the case of family@businessses that are in their third or more generation, and the company is large, complex, and requires specific management skills that are not available in the family, one can choose to retreat as a family into pure ownership and leave Operations to external specialists.

John: *Hearing your options, I have the inclination to do cherry picking, taking the best elements of all possible scenarios and throwing them together.*

Mark: *Even that scenario has a name; it is called 'the ratatouille scenario'. In a few minutes, you will understand why that is not the best of solutions.*

John: *Can't you tell me right away?*

Mark: *Because it isn't a solution at all, it is often a precursor to more final scenarios, when people are not yet sure what they want to decide. You'll learn more details later on.*

John: *Phew, let's keep it simple, please.*

Mark: *Nothing complicated, just rational scenario thinking. There is a myriad of combination possibilities but no mathematical formula exists that can show you what the best choice is. Let's go into details now and start from the other side of the continuum. After that, we will scan the intermediate scenarios.*

Scenario 2: Selling the company

In complicated family – and/or business circumstances, it can be a better and sounder decision to sell the company. Discovering that a transfer to the next generation is not beneficial for the next generation nor for the company, takes a lot of courage but in that case, selling is often the best way out.

The strong ties a family can have with its enterprise should not result in a taboo against the scenario of selling the company.

Even the mere fact of researching the possibility of this scenario may be beneficial to the family. They do not need to act upon this scenario but an open investigation through open-minded discussions with all family parties involved can lead to alternative possibilities. This exercise may strengthen the motivation within the family to find creative and constructive alternative solutions so that the family can stay in the business.

When the going really gets tough, when, e.g. conflicts within the family are thus that mediation does not seem possible or when market or financial circumstances are such that bankruptcy is imminent, selling the company may be the only solution. When there is no other possibility than the discontinuation of the family business, that very often is a traumatic experience. It will take a lot of resilience to digest this but the search for a meaningful existence outside of the Family Business realm can become a hopeful perspective. When, even in dire circumstances, people are able to stay calm, there is hope that things can change for the better. And we all know: hope is for the human mind what oxygen is for our lungs.

It is rare for a family to sell its family@business for the mere reason of cashing out. What sometimes happens is that the company is sold because the family decides to invest in a different field, for example disinvesting in chemicals and moving into the pharmaceutical industry

John and Annie

Annie: *Selling is not an option for me. Why should we? We make money, we have fun, and the family@business is thriving.*
John: *Not to forget that so many of our employees earn their living through it. And it keeps them off the streets (laughs).*
Annie: *Our children are of an age that allows them to make adult choices about what they want to do with their lives. So, we have to keep their options open concerning the family@business. Besides, Eric is totally involved already and maybe Cherly will make further steps.*
John: *Indeed. We are in a more fortunate situation than the Peterson family down the road.*
Mark: *Please explain, John.*
John: *if I remember your little introduction of this meeting correctly, we will come to that in a minute.*

Scenario 3: Interim Non-family Management

This scenario comes into play when the Next Generation is not (yet) ready to take over and they need some guidance, mentoring, and coaching or maybe they just need some extra time. There are myriad reasons why this scenario is put into place. A dramatic example of DADD is when one of the founders dies early and the children are not ready to step in.

John and Annie

John: *That's what I was just talking about, the Peterson family. The parents founded a wonderfully successful company. They also have three kids. When the kids were still in their teens, I believe the eldest daughter was only 14 years old, the father, Christopher Peterson died in a car accident. His wife Helena did not work in the company, she is a pharmacist and she didn't have a clue what the business was all about. They were all taken by surprise by this tragedy. Helena decided not to sell the company but in order to make it survive until the children were old enough to decide if they would like to step in the shoes of their Daddy, she appointed one of the top managers, Patrick, as the CEO. She also created a Board of Directors with external professionals, colleagues of her husband, people she trusted. That worked fine for about ten years until the children came of age. Their second child now is working in the company. He is still young yet a little precocious since on his 20th he already finished university. Even today, this CEO is mentoring him and the other kids to find their place in the organization.*

Annie: *Helena is a good friend of mine. She is hoping that all of her children will end up taking responsibilities in their family@business. She still misses her late husband after all these years and never remarried. She reveres Patrick who sacrificed his career for the family@business. Well, 'sacrifice' might be the wrong term because he made a fortune as CEO. I think she even made him a minority shareholder.*

Mark: *The vicissitudes of life…*

Scenario 4: Succession Within the Family

The vast majority of Family Business owners put their hopes and dreams of a succession within the family. This is very understandable: the Family Business-to a high degree- creates your identity. It is an entity that you created yourself from the tiny beginning to something that is worth being handed over to one's own children.

Yet there are many bumps and obstacles on the road toward succession. The first two questions are vital, but most often not posed:

1   Do the children want to step in?
2   Are the children competent enough?

Although these two fundamental questions are almost too obvious, many families in business simply do not dare to ask them. Unless you are afraid that they might give you an answer that you do not like ('thanks for asking but No thanks, Daddy'), the first question is rather easy and takes little courage. Just ask them their opinion and start the conversation from there.

The second question is a little more delicate. All parents, until proven otherwise, love their children and love makes one a little bit blind. This is – as we have seen in Chapter 5 – the Big Question.

Scenario 5: Management Buy-Out/in

When a family@business grows into a larger corporation with the need for a span of control that simply is too wide for the family to oversee and/or the family has not enough (capable) members to do the job and/or when the family decides that a non-family family manager is so important that her loyalty toward the family@business needs to be secured, then the external party is allowed or even invited to buy-in into the capital of the company. When in the end, there is a lack of successors interested in taking over; this may end in a management buy-out, which amounts to scenario 2. In contrast with selling the business, in this scenario, the selling family often requires that in some way or another, the family values prevail somehow. For example, a Belgian amusement park was sold to a multinational on the explicit condition that the name of the park was kept for 15 years, as well as 75% of the workforce for the coming two years.

John and Annie

Annie: *When I think of this scenario, I don't see it as a solution to our overall problem; pardon me, Mark, challenge (all laugh). But it might be worthwhile to think it over when we want to retain some of our crucial top managers.*

John: *Indeed, that is a good idea. Some of our foreign subsidiaries would benefit from a long-term commitment by the country managers.*

Mark: *Yes, this scenario is often used for these purposes.*

John: *It might even give us the freedom to allow a more or less total management buy-out when, as a family, we want to disinvest for strategic reasons. Allowing our own management to step in as owners will create us ambassadors instead of competitors.*

Scenario 6: IPO and Family@business Covenant

An Initial Public Offering (IPO) is a complicated way to float (part of) the shares of your family@business in the stock market. That way the owning family can capitalize and use that money for further expansion or for buying out family shareholders that like to disinvest.

One of the newest methods that sometimes is used when the family and the business need more flexibility and freedom for the family shareholders is the 'family@business covenant': an internal market where only family shareholders can participate. In the covenant, the rules under which family members can buy and sell shares to and from each other are agreed upon and written down. This method is especially useful for large families with large businesses that are in an advanced stadium when 'culling' the family tree is necessary.

John and Annie

John: *That is for the big boys!*

Annie: *Or girls....:)*

Mark: *Yes, this scenario is used when the company needs growth money. And/or when the need is to grow the company or the initial owners wish to dilute their ownership in turn for cash. In the days of the dotcom bubble, but even today, super-fast growers amidst the companies, use this scenario to cash in on an idea. It sometimes works, see the FANG[1] stocks, it sometimes does not work, see hundreds of forgotten listed but bust companies.*

John: *I never say "never" but this scenario will not happen in my lifetime.*

Annie: *Agreed.*

Scenario 7: Permanent Non-family Management

If the company is large enough to bear the costs of external management and there is no wish or possibility for a family member to take over the helm and there is no wish to redeem the shareholding, then this is the appropriate option. This means that the family retreats into the pure ownership, only sits on the board of directors, and hands the daily running of the corporate ship over to external specialists-confidants. In rare cases, a business family uses this option to bridge the time until a suitable family member stands up that has the capacity and will to take the helm of the family@business. This model is used by some of the most renowned family@business in the world. More so, this model is used by many of the "Hidden Champions," large organizations that are in their fourth or more generation, that hold the number one to three positions in their chosen field of business. Yet toward the outside world, there is little level of awareness of their existence. We recommend Prof. Hermann Simon's book: *Hidden champions: lessons from 500 of the world's best unknown companies.*

John and Annie

Annie: Hidden Champions, what a nice terminology and what a great idea to research those companies.
Mark: Professor Simon's works are world-class and the companies he researched are world-class.
John: That would be a nice to be a member of!
Annie: They must be as proud of their accomplishments as we are.

Scenario 8: Ratatouille or 'a Bit of Everything'

This happens when families have not decided when G1 wants to play safe, when G2 doesn't (yet) have the full courage to take over, when too many non-family stakeholders are involved and want their share in future decision-making. In some rare cases, it might be a good solution but often, too often it is the result of not daring to show true leadership by cutting the necessary knots.

Best solution when you are thinking of scenario 8, is to wait a while and see what happens next. Don't wait too long!

John and Annie

Annie: Now that was a big tour de horizon. We would and could never have thought of all those possibilities. Your explanation felt like visiting a museum of the future.
John: Amidst all of the possible scenarios, I only see the succession scenario as apt to our family. Once more, I am happy that we started this process. And we have time because Annie and myself still are very alive and kicking.
Annie: Shouldn't the children think more before they commit themselves?
Mark: Absolutely and they also have the time they need for that. If it is OK with you, I will give them the same overview as we just went through.

The John and Annie Family Meeting

This is the first time the complete family has come together for a meeting under the leadership of Mark.

Mark: Welcome, everybody. Today is a landmark moment for yourself, your family, and your family@business. You have been thinking and working for some months now around the ideas that we shared with you concerning your future.

After some social talk, Mark proceeds with the same overview that he went through with the parents a few weeks ago.

Mark: *Please keep in mind that this is just an overview so that you all share the same information. Every scenario has in itself different possibilities. There is no good or wrong scenario there are only useful possibilities that will provide you and your family and your business with the best opportunities for the future. One thing is certain, however: the more all of you agree on the chosen scenario and the more mutual effort you put into the realization of that scenario, the greater the chance that this will your sustainable solution. Any questions?*

Eric: *Yes. What about our non-family employees and other stakeholders like my wife?*

Cherly: *What happens if some of us choose a position today but over the coming time changes his or her position in the company?*

Ella: *What about family@business owners who do not work in the company?*

Mark: *All great questions. Indeed, maybe other topics need to be discussed. Like for example: how are you and/or the family are going to handle the important but delicate topic of wealth management, family charter, preconditions for your Next Gen (G3) when they want to come and work for the company, what is your collective ambition that you share with all of your employees and that is the core foundation of the company aka your 'raison d'être', and other topics that will emerge during the coming months and years.*

John: *Phew., I get dizzy from all your questions.*

Annie: *That might be true, John, and yet all these questions, however dizzying, are relevant.*

Mark: *It will be exciting to work together creating collective answers that will lay the foundations for your personal life, family life, and family@business. We will tackle all of these topics one by one as we go along in this process of succession.*

Eric: *How does this work? Do we have to first agree on everything before we take a decision? If yes, I am afraid that it is going take forever. If no, I am afraid that we will miss things of which we will be sorry afterwards.*

Mark: *The succession process that you have started is an incremental process: each decision changes the context in which the next decision will be taken. So, each step taken influences the next step. We will take care to progress slowly but steadily so everybody will have enough time to reflect before committing.*

In the months after this meeting, the family spent many hours thinking, discussing, reflecting, doubting, arguing, and finally deciding. Allowing enough time for reflection and discussion is crucial for the succession process.

First one has to consider all the possibilities, then playing around in the mind with each possible scenario, accepting that each decision closes other paths so that gradually and finally the minds ripen into decisions.

The future is unpredictable so in this succession process, we take great care to plan the future as effectively as possible. That way everybody is maximally prepared to react flexibly when faced with contingencies that cannot be foreseen. It takes courage but also wisdom to accept that in (business) life, whatever you decide, there is always a degree of uncertainty.

Note

1 Jim Cramer coined the acronym FANG in 2013 to collectively refer to the four high-growth internet stocks: Facebook, Amazon, Netflix, and Google.

Chapter 13

The Decision of a Lifetime

After in-depth consideration of all that was described in the previous chapters, after your careful yet not always comfortable study of the family@ business phases, the tools, the indicators, the exercises to help you stretch your comfort zone, the possible scenarios for the future, after all that preparation, now the time has come to decide.

For some of you, this decision is self-evident, for some of you this decision is scary, for all of you this decision is tremendously important.

Look Before You Leap

When you are G2 there is always the pressure of stepping in to become the Next Gen owner-manager. Even if your G1 parents-owners tell you: "Feel free to follow your own mission in life," you will feel the pressure of tradition, of unspoken expectancies, of feelings of duty and destiny. This is perfectly normal. Because your G1 so lovingly took care of the family@ business and because the family@business is the eldest child, there is no escape from these feelings of obligation. Accept those but do not allow yourself to be crushed by them. Take your time and the necessary distance to reflect if stepping in G1's footsteps, is what you really want with your life.

Do Not Jump to Conclusions

A word of caution: it is best not to romanticize the family@business. All too often, consultants and Family Business organizations start with the bias that the company must stay within the family. This solipsistic stance can lead to dangerous situations where children and parents – sometimes against all knowledge – remain locked up in a family@business straitjacket. This can even lead to extreme forms where the company becomes a disease that makes the people in it sick.

DOI: 10.4324/9781003194200-13

Professional service providers to family@business must develop their awareness of this cognitive bias and help business families to keep an open eye for all possible solutions, even those that go beyond the family@ business.

The solution-focused approach prefers a balancing act between what is good for the person, the family, and the company. If the outcome is that family members X and Y, however competent and motivated, do not feel certain that their future lies in the family@business, so be it.

The topic of thinking beyond the family@business is not popular, not with G1 nor with G2. Yet, driven by harsh experiences in the field, the professional service provider must have the guts to help clients not jump to conclusions. This is important for the simple reason that one cannot back off after the decision is taken and implemented without running the danger of severe damage to you and/or the family and/ or the company.

Tragedy

Disregarding the wisdom of this step can lead to tragedy as the next case shows. This family@business was into its fifth generation. The family that was in line for succession to the next generation had three children, two daughters, and a son. Tradition prescribed that the business went from father to son. The daughters both became medical specialists but the son was coerced by the pressure of five generations to step into the business. But this time, disaster struck. Very soon after the succession was completed, the son committed suicide. After his death, the grieve-stricken family found a note saying: "Please forgive me. I shamed the family. I should have talked to all of you about it but I was so ashamed. I constantly saw all the generations of successful male predecessors before me looking at me and I did not dare to talk about my anxiety that I would fail. The burden of my five generations of successful ancestors was too heavy for me. I am a loser and I cannot live with that shame. I really wanted to become a doctor like my sisters but I was too afraid to tell you. Forgive me."

Prenuptials

People marry because they love each other and then they want to translate that love into a permanent contract for the whole world to see. Nobody marries with a divorce in mind and yet, worldwide statistics show that the divorce rate is high. With divorce, especially for entrepreneurs and family@business owners, comes risk. Or one spouse can get in trouble when the others' business fails. Or the other spouse can get into trouble when the marriage fails. There is nothing romantic in a prenuptial agreement. But still, it is sound advice, especially for entrepreneurs to compliment your romantic commitment with a businesslike contract. Like all good contracts, a prenuptial is written in the hope of never having to use it. Prenuptials can have a preventive effect. And if necessary, putting the terms of the prenuptials in action can be protective for all parties involved.

Family@business Prenuptials

Of course, everybody, yourself included, is happy when the decision is taken that you join the family@business. Your parents are happy that their lifework migrates into the hands of their walking DNA. Your siblings might be happy because you take the burden. Your banker is happy because maybe, hopefully, he/she can keep your business in his/her portfolio. Your accountant is happy for the same reasons.

But your family@business consultant must have the professional guts to present you with an alternative scenario than just "eyes wide shut, full throttle ahead." Instead of jumping head over foot into the family@business, it is useful to think about what to do before and after the jump.

We developed family@business prenuptials. This is a discussion text that helps all parties involved reflect and communicate before a final decision is taken. It describes the process of a probation period, defines milestones, and offers an honorable retreat for everybody when things don't seem to work out as hoped or planned. Unlike marriage prenuptials, this is not a legal document. This is more of a gentle(wo)men's agreement. But it beats taboos and brings issues to the surface.

The Decision of Your Lifetime

Since your decision to join the family@business is a major decision with long-term consequences, being safe is better than being sorry.

Why is carefully weighing the decision to join your family@business so important? That has all to do with the fact that most children want to do their utter best, partially to please their parents, partially to fulfill their own ambitions, partially to stand up to the expectations of many other stakeholders like employees, customers, the society, etc. partially to show their loyalty toward the eldest child of the family, the family@business with which they have spent their entire life. If you don't come from a family@business, the only way to try to understand this is to "walk a mile in their shoes."

In short, joining the family@business is not the same as accepting a contract in a nonfamily business: if – for whatever reason – this goes wrong, one just steps away and moves to the next job. Stepping away from your family@business is much more complicated.

Before you Commit

If you are not 110% sure (yet) but you still want to give it a try, you can use the following tools to create a safe environment for you, the family, and the business before fully committing:

1 Discuss the consequences of a possible "no" before you give it a try.
2 Make sure that you have a backup plan if the decision is a no-go.
3 Communicate enough with your family beforehand so that, whatever the outcome of your decision process will be, your family relationships remain intact.
4 Negotiate a probation period with G1 in which you can get a taste of the family@business.
5 Fulfill your probation period in a spot in the Family@business where both the company and your self-esteem cannot be harmed if you step out.
6 Make sure all crucial stakeholders realize that you are testing the waters during this probation period.
7 Choose a relevant function in the Family@business where you can experience how it really feels to work with your family while testing your professional capacities.
8 Have the courage to say "not yet" or "thank you but no, thank you."

After You Commit

When you feel confident to go for it, then and only then say "yes" to full commitment. When you say "yes," unleash your passion and energy and immerse yourself fully into the family@business.
   The following guidelines can help you:

1 Succession, or more precisely, taking over, is a process and not an event so: one small step at the time.
2 Create clear goals for yourself and make these into flexible guidelines.
3 Leave the "low hanging fruit" challenges for your co-workers and tackle the more difficult challenges in order to gain credibility through your hard work.
4 Your name is on the letterhead: work harder than the people around you.
5 Take personal responsibility for your failures and learn from them.
6 Altruism reaps greater rewards than egocentrism: share and celebrate successes, both your own but especially those of your co-workers.
7 Enjoy it, show your enjoyment, and include others in it.

Marathon, Not Sprint

Your work as Next Gen probably will last you a generation. Since nobody can run a marathon at sprint speed, the advice is to go slow, especially when you are in a hurry.

With the Next Gen in place, the time has come to include all the other stakeholders.

Chapter 14

The Dance of the Stakeholders

In the previous chapters, you have learned what the necessary preliminaries are for a family@business when the time has come for the next generation. The Founders-Owners and the Next Gen did the necessary preparatory work, as you have seen in the previous chapters. This process obviously is not linear. Like all of the succession processes, it is incremental and stochastic: it proceeds with steps that follow each other in an unpredictable manner. Sometimes there is a standstill, sometimes there are giant leaps, sometimes it is as if nothing happens, and then suddenly major changes emerge.

Until now, the accent was fully on what needs to happen within the family, the dance of the shareholders.

In the coming chapters, more accents are on the business side of the succession process. When preparing for succession, the most logical order is to start with the family and, when they deem that they are ready, involve the organization. Do not think that one can draw a mathematically precise line where one part ends and the other starts. Sometimes these developments run synchronously, sometimes one after the other, sometimes in overlap, sometimes in disconnect.

Who Is Where?

Stakeholders come in many colors. For this book, we concentrate on the people who are closely connected to the family@business.

The classic tool to chart all relevant stakeholders in a family@business is the Three Circle Model by Tagiuri and Davis from 1982.

DOI: 10.4324/9781003194200-14

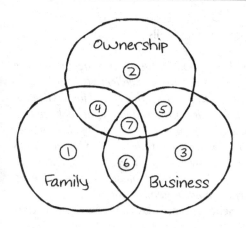

1. Family members who don't work in the business and don't own shares.
2. Non-family owners who don't work in the business.
3. Non-family members who work in the business and don't own shares.
4. Family owners who don't work in the business.
5. Non-family owners who work in the business.
6. Family members who work in the business and don't own shares.
7. Family owners who work in the business.

When you study the three overlapping circles you will learn that there are seven possible positions. This Three Circle Model, like the family genogram, gives an almost immediate overview of where everybody is situated and it prevents forgetting relevant parties.

Dynamics for the Three Circles

It is good to realize that in your own family@business, over time the three circles can vary in size. When you are a small startup company, the chance is high that there are only owning family members working in the company. This brings all stakeholders together in position 7. When you are a large, multigenerational, and diversified family@business with several family branches and lots of employees, most likely position number 3 will hold the most people.

Shareholders and Stakeholders

All shareholders are stakeholders but not all stakeholders are shareholders.

Stakeholders come in many colors: internal stakeholders (employees, in-laws, ...) and external stakeholders (customers, suppliers, business partners, banks, the local community, the world, ...).

Depending on your local legislation and marriage contract, spouses can be shareholders and/or stakeholders.

Stakeholder Stewardship

Stakeholders are the life and blood of every organization. In the old days, one used to talk about "stakeholder management" but stakeholders are far too precious to be merely managed. They deserve far better. So, whoever is responsible for conducting this pulsing orchestra toward success needs stewardship skills that top mere management skills.

> *"In stewardship theory, the model of man is based on a steward whose behavior is ordered such that pro-organizational, collectivistic behaviors have higher utility than individualistic, self-serving behaviors. Given a choice between self-serving behavior and pro-organizational behavior, a steward's behavior will not depart from the interests of his or her organization. A steward will not substitute or trade self-serving behaviors for cooperative behaviors. Thus, even where the interests of the steward and the principal are not aligned, the steward places higher value on cooperation than defection (terms found in game theory)"*
>
> Davis, J.H., Schoorman, F.D. & Donaldson, L.1997

In plain English, this means: people like to be part of a bigger whole; they like to do their utter best for the sake of something bigger than themselves and they like to do this together with other people. If treated correctly and respectfully, people do not need control, monitoring, external incentive nor bribery to do their paid work. They choose not to exchange time for money but are intrinsically motivated to do the best job possible. Stewards identify themselves with the organization and use their personal power to create the best possible collectivistic culture with an appropriate power distance between the different levels in the company.

The classic method Plan-Do-Check-Adjust becomes Plan-Do-**Trust**. Trust creates engagement and commitment. Engagement interwoven with commitment interwoven with trust forges a resilient network system that can withstand the heat of negativity at all times.

Family@business Goes for the Long and Sustainable Haul

Some large (multi) national and/or listed companies are (all too often) driven by short-term gains, stock price movements and bonus systems can create a pervert effect on management.

In contrast, most family@business manages their business for the long term. Professors Danny Miller and Isabella Le Breton-Miller have shown in their important bestselling book "Managing for the long run," what the key elements are that explain why family@businessses are more successful over a longer period of time. They call this the 4-C-model: continuity, community, connection, and command.

Continuity points to the long-term vision that forms their fundamental mission. Continuity in leadership is equally important. Their research shows that on average a generation leads the company for 24 years before the next generation is ready for takeover. *Community* stands for loyalty to their employees. A family@business often grows into a tight community where long-time co-operation, driven by shared values, creates powerful teams. Informal structures and the taking of initiative are more valued than job titles. *Connection* stands for loyalty toward and warm relationships with business partners and customers. *Command* stands for short decision lines where innovation is not hampered by management layers. It also stands for diversity in the management team.

More and more family businesses are emphasizing the importance of sustainability, circular economy, cradle-to-grave manufacturing, and environmental awareness, which by definition is long-term. We met a family@business where the only son did his studies in the UK. When he was ready to come back home and start working at his father's business, he refused: "I will not work for you as long as you do not clean up the company and organize it conform to modern environmental standards." Daddy complied!

The Quintuplet People, Planet, Passion, Profit, and Pleasure

There was a time when it was all about the money so Profit was the deity. Then People were added. Later the Planet became important and during the recent years, (family) business understood that Passion is needed to go for the long haul. Pleasure makes the cocktail so much tastier.

In which order the 5P's (People, Planet, Profit, Pleasure, Passion) come depends on the choices that each family@business makes. Over time and in synchrony with the developing strategy of the company, this order can change.

Quintuple P-exercise:

Explain the Five P's to everybody and ask yourself, your family, your (top) management, and your employees in what order they think and feel that for your family@business, they put each of the P's.

Mind you: this can be a "from 1 to 5" linear order, it can be a drawing. Use your creativity.

Everybody does this exercise in private. Later on, you make the results visible to everyone so that everyone can see how their team members see the order. Then you organize an open discussion and draw conclusions as a team.

Most family@businesses put people on the first rank. As a direct result, or perhaps as a direct cause, family@business people are naturally more inclined to be intrinsically motivated. After all, their job is not just a job. Their job is a means to carry the legacy of their predecessors into the future. Moreover, their job gives meaning.

Family@business people work with the people they love or at least with people with whom they have a biological bond: DNA. It is only natural that they take care of their family.

It is just as obvious that they take care of their employees who often, after many years of collaboration and after many life events together, have become a non-family family. The business, its survival, and prosperity are often a bigger goal than the money involved. Money then becomes a tool and not a goal.

> *Human development, as an approach, is concerned with what I take to be the basic development idea: namely, advancing the richness of human life, rather than the richness of the economy in which human beings live, which is only a part of it.*
> *Amartya Sen, Nobel Prize Economy 1988*

John and Annie

Annie: *Don't you think the time has come to talk to our employees, John?*

John: *Absolutely. We have done the necessary preparations within the family. But what would we be without our people?*

Annie: *Not to forget our customers and suppliers.*

John: *Just last week, one of our oldest suppliers -she is about my age- told me that she is thinking about stepping down. She said that she already had a meeting with her top management to explain her plans for the future. "I had to act swiftly," she said, "because rumors were out in the company that people started feeling uncomfortable and even anxious for their future." Then she asked me what our plans are.*

Annie: *Well, I can understand that. Employees have to think about their own future too. They have responsibilities towards their own families.*

John: *OK, I will ask Eric to organize a meeting with our top management. This can be done when everybody is in the country for the quarterly review meeting next week. Eric can announce that besides the usual meeting, we will organize an additional "Prepare for the Future" meeting where the family will be present.*

The Management Team of Solution Builders International

CFO Muriel
  Head Marketing Alice
  HR and Legal Lillian

Country managers Bruce, Gunther, Alessia, Jacques, Chen
General Manager Jerry
Investment manager Mony
Business Unit managers Monika, Andrea, Patrick, Rebecca

The Management Team Meets up the Evening Before, Scene at the Bar

Jerry (GM):	*Welcome, I am glad you all made it in time. We all have had the announcement of an additional "Prepare for the Future" meeting.*
Bruce (CM):	*Do you know what this will be about? It left me guessing.*
Chen (CM):	*To be frank, I am a little worried. I only work in the company for two years and have spent most of my time building the organization in my country. I hope that stopping this investment will not be part of the future. My personal future depends on it.*
Alessia (CM):	*I don't think that will happen. That is not the style of the family. If truly tough decisions were needed in the past, with repercussions on personnel or subsidies or whatever, John always dealt with it personally and in the most open manner. They would not announce a meeting with every important stakeholder, John would call you up and meet with you within 24 hours of his call.*
Jerry (GM):	*Besides, if such a thing would be the case, I would know.*
Chen (CM):	*And share your knowledge with us? What if you are told not to do that?*
Jerry (GM):	*Dear Chen, I understand your worry. But like Alessia said, that is not the style of the house. Maybe you know more, Alice. You work here since the very beginning and you are the confidante of the family.*
Alice:	*Well, I am glad you worry. That shows your commitment. And no, I was not told what it will be about either. Of course, I asked Annie but she just said "you'll see." She was smiling though.*
Muriel (CFO):	*You all know the numbers since I sent you the collated overview of all departments, business units, and subsidiaries. Besides, you know the numbers for your own department because you made them. And financially, we are sound. Business is going strong.*
Lillian:	*I work here for almost ten years. I can understand your worries as country managers. You are far from HQ, so you*

	only catch up with the buzz when you are here. I have total confidence that it will be something constructive.
Gunther (CM):	*The same goes for me. I am the oldest of our gang here. Use your imagination for a bit. The title of the meeting says it all. It is about the future. Considering John and Annie's age and give the fact that Eric has successfully worked himself through many departments, my guess it that is what it will be about.*
Jerry (GM):	*That is exactly my guess too. I propose that we have one more drink and then go to bed. Chen and Bruce have a jetlag to kill and we all need to be fresh tomorrow.*

The Management Team Meets With the Family

After breakfast, the meeting starts at 09:00. Present are John, Annie, Cherly, and Eric. Ella is excused because she is attending a medical conference.

John:	*Most welcome everybody. I trust you had a safe trip, a nice dinner yesterday, and a good night's sleep. Annie will shortly explain our agenda for today. After lunch, we have scheduled two extra hours of rest, especially for Chen and Bruce who traveled the most time zones.*
Chen:	*Thank you, John. I am sure Bruce also appreciates your concern.*
Bruce:	*Yep, thanks.*
Annie:	*Welcome on behalf of the family. During lunch, we will have time to chat. I want to know how you and your families are doing. But, John, go ahead.*
John:	*Today's meeting is different from our regular business meetings. We called it "Prepare for the Future," which is of course what we always do. But this meeting has a different purpose to it. You all know the history of our company. You all know how important the company is to Annie and myself. And Annie and myself know how much the company means to all of you. You all are the company.*
Annie:	*The last months we have been discussing amongst family how we see their future in and for the company. We have made some emotional, psychological, financial, and fiscal scenarios. We have made some strategic exercises. But we need you in this. As shareholders, we need you as stakeholders to feel maximally involved.*
John:	*We worked with family@business consultants to prepare. You will meet them in a later stadium. But today, I want to keep it amongst us, our family, and you, our non-family family. Let me start with clarity: the company will stay in the family, we will*

proceed on the same growth path as the last years, we will not make changes concerning external financing, we are not for sale nor are we interested in an IPO, fusion or whatever. We will go our own way like we have successfully done in the last twenty years. We keep adapting to the changing circumstances in our different markets. We keep a sharp eye on macroeconomic developments and we will continue our business initiatives while staying in line with the work of our risk management unit.

Annie: *In short, we keep changing while staying the same.*

John: *And we invite all of you to keep participating in this T.E.A.M work. Now, you all remember how you were selected to come and work with our company.*

Alice: *I remember as if it was yesterday.*

Mony: *I remember that also. First, there was that terrible assessment where I was rejected by the assessment consultant. Still, John wanted to see me because he had learned about my previous experience as an investment manager for a large fund. (Towards the others in the room) He practically dissected me with his questions. After an hour or so, he suddenly took the assessment file, threw it in the bin, and asked me when I would like to start.*

Muriel: *He did the same with me. He grilled me with questions about the minute details of my work at my previous job. Just before we shook hands to settle our agreement, he told me: "Muriel, you will become the CFO of the group. I don't care that you are so young, I don't care that you are pregnant. But I do demand that you will always be critical towards whomever and whatever you find that needs criticism. If I ever find out that you keep back your criticism because of company politics, you will be in trouble."*

Chen: *Two years ago, I was anxious because I really wanted this job. It was a big adventure for me, starting a subsidiary from zero. John told me that the key to my success would be to marry a critical mind to an entrepreneurial stance: better make mistakes than do nothing or worse, shying away from things that might fail.*

John: *I like your stories. That is the spirit in our team and it has to stay like that. It is one of the bases for your personal success and therefore for our common success. The rest is just hard work.*

Annie: *And a bit of luck at the correct time.*

John: *We have embarked on a journey of management- and inheritance succession. We will share with you which steps we already have taken, which will be the next steps and how we expect you to contribute to this process. By doing this, we are*

|Annie:| *securing the future of the company and therefore the future of all of us.* |

securing the future of the company and therefore the future of all of us.

Annie: *Before we do that, can I add something, John? You were talking about criticism, no company politics and no shying away from things delicate. I would like to be more specific and I am sure that for all of you it will be things that you already have heard many times. More, all of you have proven over time that you fit into our company culture. For now: please keep a critical mind and heart but use your criticism with respect for the other. Since we are becoming a larger company, we cannot avoid a certain level of administrative bureaucracy. Please help us to keep it minimal so that we continue to work in the Plan-Do-Trust mode. And maybe most important of all: speak freely. Over the years we have proven that speaking freely but respectfully with each other about whatever you deem useful, always bears fruit in a positive way.*

Eric: *Sorry to interrupt you but I think this is crucial. You know that it is my ambition to learn a lot more from you and from my parents. You also know that I have the ambition to take up my leadership mandate in the future. You know that I can be a little square when dealing with people, especially when I am stressed. In the succession work that we did with our family@ business consultants, a lot became clear to me. I am doing my best to change my style. And I need all the help I can get with this. This help can only come from you, my colleagues.*

Annie: *In the coming months, we embark on the next legs of the succession process and we need you all to speak up if there are things that you find important to take in to account or if there are evolutions that worry you.*

John: *Well said, Annie. Can I add one more thing?*

Jerry (GM): *I will say it in your place: trust is OK but trust comes with results. (all laugh)*

External Stakeholders

At the end of the day, customers and clients pay the bills. Service providers like accountants, ICT specialists, lawyers, psychologists, family@business consultants, scientists, etc. facilitate operations. Strategic partners like suppliers, financial institutes, research organizations; government agencies, etc. create the biotope in which the family@business can thrive. The (local, national, and international) community combined with the vicissitudes of micro- and macroeconomic evolution, form the stage on and according to which the family@business acts.

The In-Between Is Essential

The working relationship between shareholders, management, stewards, and stakeholders are vital to the company's health, growth, and – ultimately – survival.

Change Is the Only Constant

Having a clear vision of who are your stakeholders is necessary but not enough. Because we live and work in an ever-changing world, there is only one constant: change. Therefore, one needs a strategy that continuously monitors, informs, and updates you about the ever-developing changes in your stakeholder and shareholder relationship network.

Differentiate Between Stakeholders

There is this strange habit of treating everybody in the same way, whatever their differences. Prof. Dr. Hans Galjaard taught us: "The greatest in-equality is the equal treatment of unequal's." In this light, we advocate the use of realistic differentiation between stakeholders whereby all deserve equal respect yet not all need the same amount of time and effort. The challenge is: dare to differentiate.

Ambassadors

Happy shareholders create happy stakeholders. Happy stakeholders create ambassadors for the family@business. Happy ambassadors create long-lasting and sustainable business. Long-lasting and sustainable business creates happy shareholders. Happy shareholders ...

By now, the Founders-Owners have taken care of the future for their non-family employees and for their many employees. Now the time has come to reflect on how the Founders-Owners can take care of themselves when they gradually let go their life's work.

Chapter 15

G1 How to Let Go after Succession?

Starting a business is a step into the unknown. That is an exciting look into the future. When the time has come for the Next Gen to be ready to take over and the founders can take a step back, it is also exciting. But now, by definition, the view of the future is much shorter. Instead of building, now the time has come to let go.

John and Annie

Annie: *So far, So good. I am pleased that we have taken plenty of time to look at the decisions for the future from all possible angles. As a family, we have had enough conversations, so that we now all have the confidence to continue.*

John: *What satisfies me is how our management has taken responsibility in this process. But what really satisfies me is the confidence they have in the direction of the Next Gen.*

Annie: *Now it's our turn again.*

John: *What do you mean?*

Annie: *Well, my dear husband, the challenge for us is to take a step back, let go and trust that everything will be all right.*

John: *Right. I realize that it will be difficult for me to stand back and sit on my hands if they do things differently from what I would do.*

Annie: *I won't always be there to correct you.*

John: *We simply don't have any experience with this.*

Annie: *No, but we have experience with asking for help. Let's call Mark and see if he can help.*

John and Annie make an appointment with Mark, their family@business consultant and they explain their predicament.

Mark: *Thanks for calling me. Do I understand you when you say that you*

DOI: 10.4324/9781003194200-15

*want more information about the next phase, namely preparing for a
step back?*

Annie: *Correct.*

Mark: *This is a very important phase for Founder-Owners. If this step is not
handled in the right way, people will regret it afterwards.
Congratulations on having taken this into account in advance. I will
share all relevant information with you. Don't worry about
remembering it, I'll give you an article I wrote so you can read it
again after our meeting.*

Now Mark takes his time to share and discuss the following information
with John and Annie.

Why Is Letting Go So Difficult for Every G1?

1 Growing a sustainable Family Business is a lifelong task for a Founder-
Owner.

That task sometimes can feel like a burden, and yet it also is
comfortable. Because this task, along with all the pressure it brings,
demands that the Founder-Owner has a laser-sharp focus on this one,
albeit very complex task. No other distractions are allowed in his Zen-
like concentration.

2 The company absorbs your time and energy.

Whatever he/she does, thinks, feels, it all needs to be directed at the
demands of daily business issues, problems, and challenges. This focus
gives direction and meaning to his life. Successful Founders-Owners are
driven and passionate people with long-term goals in their minds.

3 The company gives immediate and constant feedback.

Luckily, they get some help from the company itself. Whenever their
attention slackens a little, there is an immediate feedback from the
company in terms of lesser results, dwindling quality, unsatisfied
customers, and what have you. This feedback keeps them alert.

4 You are your company and your company is you.

The enormous attention and energy that a business unendingly
demands, results in a strong identification with the business.

For the G1 transferring partner, especially in the case of a Founder-
Owner, the Family Business is the eldest child, his/her lifework, and the
primary – very often the only – focus of attention. He/she lives in it,
through it, from it, and with it. His/her identity as a person often
coincides with the position as Owner and Founder. Uncertainty about
the business is inseparably connected to uncertainty about what will
happen as a person when he/she no longer is the top dog in the company
and its network.

Change is Inevitable

Nothing is as unchangeable as change. So, there is always a time to come and a time to go. When the time to go has come, it can be done in different ways. The style that the Founder-Owner chooses is already indicated by the words he chooses to use. He can be speaking of "leave it to" or "transferring." Same goes for the successor: she can choose the words "taking over' or 'accepting the transfer." The words indicate a passive or an active style.

There is a fierce debate about which style is the best but one thing is sure: succession happens sooner or later, voluntary or forced, active or passive. What the best way is, cannot be defined by management gurus or scientific books but by what works best for this family and this company.

Two Important Worries

The two main worries that may cause procrastination for the Owner-Founder in this phase of the process of succession are:

1   How does he/she/they see their personal future?
2   How will his/her company operate under new leadership?

These are major worries. Founders-entrepreneurs are by nature more do-ers than thinkers while these challenges require a lot of thinking (and feeling). Plus, these challenges require that one fights the taboo resting on one's own mortality and uncertainty about oneself.

So, it is necessary to create a mental image of how the personal is separated from the business is an important preparation before you can take steps in that direction. We offered you a roadmap to do this in Chapter 6 where you find a list of best practices and tips.

Secondly, the Next Gen does not have a proven track record of being proficient in taking the lead over the company as a whole. At the same time, the Founder-Owner will vividly remember the challenges, difficulties, and failures that he/she has encountered while building the company. In this phase of the process, you can hear G1 worrying and doubting: "will they be able to cope? What if it goes wrong? Is it not too early to put so much weight on their shoulders? Are they capable?"

The Essential Skill

When you are transferring your family business, the biggest skill you need is the ability to let go. Actually, this skill is double-edged. It requires the skill to let go, both on a personal level and on a business level.

This double-edged challenge stems from the fact that very often the Founder-Owner feels that his person *is* his business and that his business *is* his person. Only by letting go of both elements, the space opens in which you can find other fulfillments in life.

Letting Go is a Complex Process

At the end of the career of the Founder-Owner there are a lot of aspects that need consideration. Issues that play are financial, legal, emotional, psychological, and relational.

Financial and Legal Aspect

However difficult – and even threatening – it may feel to let go of the ownership and the financial security that comes with it, still, this element often is the easiest in the complex of processes. Most Founder-Owners have a personal financial buffer by that time plus there are many financial and banking techniques that make this transition feasible.

Our experience in succession dossiers shows us that talking about financial aspects, however difficult it may be in the beginning, often is a good theme to start with for these reasons:

- Talking finance and money is core business for entrepreneurs who otherwise would never have made it this far;
- It helps to overcome the counterproductive fear that all things money-wise should be and remain a secret;
- It frees parents of the idea that their children will be spoiled if they know how much the company is worth and how much they will inherit;
- It shows openness toward the next generation and they feel trusted that their parents openly talk about financial matters;
- Financial security for the Owner-Founder's future is of paramount importance if all parties involved want to make sure that the family business's future is theirs and that Daddy will not stick around to keep a watchful eye out because he needs the finances;
- These discussions – that are often rather technical – prepare the ground for discussion about the following more intangible but maybe even more essential aspects.

The legal side is easy: you can buy the knowledge from technical experts.

Beware: to think that succession is only a question of financial and legal matters and refuse to take care of other aspects, is shortsighted and is likely to cause failure or at least great difficulties in the long term.

Emotional Aspect

Daring to admit to oneself, and others, that it is emotionally hard to let go of the company that has been the core of one's existence for so many years is much harder. Allowing feelings of anxiety, stress, uncertainty, self-doubt, sadness often is "not done" in the tough business world. There still is the idea that showing emotions is dangerous because others might see you as weak and/or take advantage. But allowing your emotions to show, does not diminish your strength as a businessman.

Psychological Aspect

Facing the fact that a great deal of self-esteem and self-confidence stems from the position that you have in your Family Business and not from within yourself, seems to be taboo in the macho world of founding entrepreneurs. Letting go of that position and finding other sources of self-esteem and self-confidence is a tough challenge.

Relational Aspect

Going through life as the Founder-Owner of a Family Business has a high social standing. Your spouse and family share in that social perception. Your position has a big influence on all of your social relations: you are Mr. and Mrs. Family Business. Yet stepping down from this position may result in big changes in that social standing. On top of that, it can be scary to realize that your social network can suddenly become small when you are no longer active.

Confronted with all these aspects, the worst one can do is pretending as if all these changes do not exist. Giving in to the fear that one is seen as a weakling because you experience difficulties with all these changes, is counterproductive. All human beings unavoidably have to go through transitional phases. This is part of life and part of business life.

Of course, the next generation still needs your experience and expertise. An often-used scenario is that the Founder-Owner steps out of his operational role and becomes Chairman of the Board. Gradually the Chairman position will become a symbolic position and then time has come to fully let go.

Is letting go difficult?
Yes!
Is letting go an impossible task?
No!
Is it a skill that can be learned? YES!

Principle 1: Grab Something Else Instead

Stepping back from your Family Business after a life of hard work and full commitment leaves you with a lot of time and energy on your hand. If you do not take care, you might stumble into the well-known "black hole." To avoid this, it is best to grab onto something new while you let go of the family business. This new thing can be almost anything, as long as it fits with you and you commit yourself to it: grandchildren, golfing, rediscovering your relationship, classic cars, joining a club, philanthropy, studying Buddhism, travel, ...

Imagine this transition as a process of fading out/in. The new will help you deal with the emotions that accompany taking distance and then gradually saying goodbye to your life in business.

Very soon you will build a new identity in this new phase of your life. You will also notice that a complete new social network opens itself when you focus the time and energy that you used to spend on the family business, on new horizons.

Principle 2: Look at Your Personal Future

What also is very helpful is to realize that you will be forever the Founder even after you no longer will be the Owner. Then your company that has been your eldest child will become your "eldest grandchild" for whom others will take the responsibility.

If you do this wisely, your inspiration, vision, and values are likely to remain active in the company you have left behind. You can now relax and enjoy from a distance how your successors build on your heritage and how they (re) built the Family Business that suits them and new times.

Ten Tips to Help You Let Go

1 Accept that change is an inevitable part of life.
2 Realize that you are not alone: because change is so difficult for most people, letting go is equally difficult for everybody.
3 Hopelessly clinging causes cramps!
4 Letting go is a process that takes time.
5 Letting go becomes easier if you can take something else in hand.
6 Talk about it with your partner, friends, children, trusted advisors, business colleagues but also with people who have gone through this process.
7 Give yourself an explicit assignment to become interested in things that have nothing to do with your family business.
8 Accept that you will encounter difficult moments in which you will feel lost. If this happens, try not to panic, allow yourself a temporary

standstill, focus your attention on novel things, and/or allow yourself to float for a while on the liberating banality of daily life.

9   Offer yourself all the time that you need for this because it cannot be forced.

10 Keep in mind that life is too short to not enjoy it to the fullest: Vita Brevis, Ars longa (Aristotle).

John and Annie

John: *Wow, what a lecture! Very enlightening. Much of what you have just explained has never occurred to me before.*

Mark: *That's why we, family@business consultants, were invented in the first place. (All laughing)*

Annie: *We are happy for your article. This gives us food for thought. I realize that at this stage it is more about taking care of ourselves and our personal future.*

Now all generations are ready to take the next steps that will help launch both the family and the business toward a successful next generation.

Intermezzo

The next two chapters, Chapter 16 on the governance and Chapter 17 on the management of the family@business consecutively describe the crucial tools that are the foundations upon which the future of the family@business and of all of its stakeholders are built.

Family members might want to read Chapter 16 on family@ business governance tools first. Managers and non-family professionals might want to read Chapter 17 on business management tools first.

In the real-life of a family@business, these tools are developed and deployed simultaneously. It is therefore only for didactic reasons that the tools are described linearly here.

In addition, a linear medium such as a book offers few opportunities to describe the dynamics of all these processes.

Sometimes they're consecutive:

- G2 can only take steps forward when G1 agrees,
- the family best takes preparatory steps before the employees are involved,
- Next Gen scenarios preferably are explored before a decision is taken, etc.

Sometimes they are simultaneous:

- Discussions with the internal stakeholders and especially the top management about their and the family's future run parallel with the development of the business,
- management and strategy tools are put to work while the competencies of the Next Gen are honed,
- G2 gently steps to the foreground while G1 gradually moves back and this fading in/out happens parallel with changes in the governance of the family@business, etc.

Moreover, each family@business case is as different as our fingerprints so the timing of deployment of all these tools needs to fit with the specific needs of this particular family@business.

Chapter 16

Three Family@business Governance Tools

Every family@business is a body established and managed in accordance with corporate law in the legal systems of various countries. The specific rules differ per country and per state or province. These rules also differ according to the legal structure in which the company is incorporated. However important, for these reasons, the technical details of legal, financial, and fiscal corporate constructions are out of the scope of this book.

The Governance of a Family@business Is Complex

The reason for this complexity is simple: many layers are operational at the same time and need to be coordinated with each other. Without wanting to be exhaustive, let's take a look at the most important of them.

The *shareholders' agreement* ensures that all owners are safe from unexpected events, be it a hostile takeover or, at worst, a co-owner who puts his shares up for sale without pre-consultation.

The *Board of Directors* is the governing body of the company. Through it, the wishes, hopes, and dreams of the owning family are translated into the business strategy. This strategy is the guideline for the work of the top management and their collaborators.

The Board of Directors steers and supervises the *Executive Direction Committee*. The members of the direction committee, i.e. the top management can execute their strategy with minimal interference by the family because directors, executives, and family are aligned thanks to their Collective Ambition (Chapter 17).

Often there is a functional overlap between the two bodies, e.g. a family member is an owner, board member, and director. As long as the terms and conditions of the decision-making process are transparent and as long

DOI: 10.4324/9781003194200-16

as there are enough checks and balances that guarantee a correct legal operation, that does not need to be a problem.

When the company grows into phase 3 (Chapter 2) and certainly when the Next Gen steps on board, it becomes useful, necessary, and effective to create a full functioning board of directors. The complexity becomes thus that it is advisable that external board members are put into position. In view of the transition process toward the Next Gen, when the company enters phase 4 and certainly in phase 5, the position of the Founder-Owner typically moves from CEO to chairman of the board before leaving the family@business scene entirely.

The task for every organization is to design the corporate governance structure that fits the best with the needs of the family, the business, and the staff, obviously in line with the legal and fiscal requirements of the country where the family@business is operational. For all these layers, efficacy stems from the T.E.A.M-idea: Together Each Achieves More!

Three Family@business Governance Tools

In order to allow the family and company to navigate the turbulent waters of the future in a flexible and adaptive way, the following interventions are helpful:

- Jointly draft a common text that encompasses all matters important to the functioning of the family in the company.
- Create a communication platform where discussions on all possible topics can take place,
- Initiate a leadership style that underpins the cohesion and connection within the family.

Three major tools are available for this:

1. The *Family Charter* is the document describing all the family's agreements on sensitive issues. This is – metaphorically – the code for this family.
2. The *Family Forum* is the meeting where all matters of family and business can be safely discussed.
3. *Family Stewardship* is the tool that keeps the family connected with each other and with all other stakeholders in the coming decades.

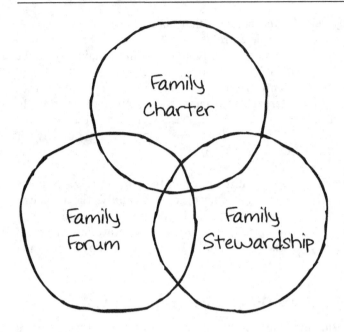

1 Family Charter

A family charter is a document that describes all the elements that the family members deem important in order to streamline and maintain their future cooperation.

As with the Collective Ambition, the iterative process that leads up to the final document is much more important than the final document itself.

The final Family Charter is as unique as each individual; family and family@business are unique. As an instrument that guides the way the family members relate to each other in the business context, it can only emerge through open discussions within the family. Beware: this takes time and effort. When the Family Charter is ready and agreed upon by everybody, you will get the impression: "Can it be that simple? Did we need so much time and effort to obtain this as a result?" If the answer is yes, then you can rest assured that the family charter you crafted is the family charter you need.

The topics that are covered in a Family charter differ by family but the following components are usually included:

- family and corporate values
- rules of conduct within the family
- rules of conduct within the company
- objectives of the company
- expected contributions by every family member

- method of dealing with changing circumstances
- career possibilities
- training requirements
- family-in-law
- dividend policy
- investment policy
- remuneration policy
- leadership of the family
- leadership of the company
- frequency of family meetings
- setting the agenda, ...

In order to lose no time or energy, it can be helpful to work with a family@ business consultant with experience in this field. That way, if and when conflicts arise, these can be processed in positive manner.

The John and Annie Family Meet Mark

The family asks Mark what, in his experience is the best way forward when creating a family charter.

Mark: *As I already explained to you, the content of a family charter is totally up to the needs of your family. I gave you a list of potential issues that often find a spot in a family charter, but it is absolutely not mandatory. A family charter is a non-legal document. It is more of a commonly generated manifesto that morally binds all involved.*

John: *How do we begin?*

Mark: *Best practice is that everybody of the family makes a list of which issues and topics that they want to be addressed. Then we come together for an open discussion. At that moment you will notice that some details can be captured in more generic terms that will prevent you from writing a book. (Smiles)*

Eric: *OK. Actually, my list is already done. Maybe we win time and proceed faster if we start from my list.*

Mark: *You know, Mark, how the saying goes: if you are in a hurry, go slow. Now, I know from experience that preparing your personal list and then discussing it together, seems slow but in reality, it goes fast.*

Eric: *OK, you are the expert.*

Two weeks later, Saturday, 10:00 at the office. Everybody presents his or her list. Mark writes down issues that are connected on separate flip-overs. After a few hours, the general structure of the family charter is starting to become visible.

Mark: *As far as I see, the following categories seem important for you as a family. What are our family values that we want to carry towards the future? How are the general objectives of the company linked to those values? What general rules of conduct towards each other, the employees and external stakeholders do we prefer? What do we expect from the Next Gen in terms of education and experience before they can join the company? What is the standpoint towards the in-laws? What is our core financial objective (a non-exhaustive list: dividend policy, selling of shares, investment policy)? How will we support sustainable entrepreneurship? Does everybody feel that the items on your personal list have been taken into account?*

Ella: *What about social responsibility and philanthropy?*

Mark: *If everybody agrees, let us add those too. On a separate flip-over or do you see them connected to one of the other topics?*

Ella: *Best separate, I think.*

Mark: *Good work. I will make pictures of each flip-over and email them to you. I count nine different categories. My suggestion is that each chooses two categories and then work in pairs on a text that describes the content of the category.*

Ella: *I take the philanthropy and social responsibility topics that I added. I think this can be one category. Mom, would you like to work with me?*

Annie: *Sure, Dear. Let us add the family values category.*

Eric: *Can I work on the financial objectives and how those connect to our values as a family? That way, there is a double vision by two teams on this topic. For me, this is maybe one of the most crucial foundations for our company and for our family. Cherly, would you like to join me?*

Cherly (amazed):   *Well, hmm, sure Eric, thank you.*

Annie: *Good move, son.*

John: *Annie, why don't we take the general rules of conduct and the expectation for the Next Gen?*

Annie: *There is the delicate topic on the involvement of the in-laws. In my opinion, you children must take the lead in this. Maybe you should pre-discuss this amongst the three of you.*

Mark: *That leaves the topic of sustainable entrepreneurship, which is a good thing because this topic probably is an amalgamation of all the other categories. Let's wrap up for today. When do we meet again?*

After the children have left, John and Annie come sit with Mark.

Annie: *I am happy, John, that you were able to let the kids to most of the work. I was a little apprehensive that you would take the lead in this exercise and that the children, out of respect, would not speak their minds.*

John: *Me too, I am happy that they took the lead. Even Cherly added a lot of input. And since there was no tension between her and Eric, Ella did not have to intervene. Plus, I kept my mouth shut most of the time. Believe me, it took some effort to sit on my hands.*

Mark: *You both did a great job, congratulations. I can imagine that it feels good to notice the children taking leadership in this exercise and that they give each other space.*

Annie: *I liked the way you restrained Eric in the beginning of the meeting.*

Mark: *And Eric took it well, which is progress for him.*

The John and Annie Family Charter

After some months of work, meetings in pairs, emailing the intermediate results back and forth, discussing, correcting, adapting, and rewriting, the family agreed upon the following charter. When you study their result, you will see that all the above categories are incorporated.

Soft and hard, together each achieves more.

In this Family Charter, the John and Annie family describe our family and business values. These values are captured in the words: **Caring–Sharing–Daring.**

   We also express how we want to behave towards each other and all other stakeholders. It is a common manifesto that describes our entrepreneurship and stewardship and defines the outlines for our future.

1. The members of the John and Annie family take great pride in the tenacity, flexibility, and entrepreneurial courage that is the foundation of our family and family@business. Respect combined with courteousness and integrity create a climate of loyalty that goes beyond the family.
2. We are passionate about hard work and results while we are soft with each other without being softies.
3. We treat each other like we want to be treated ourselves.
4. We strongly believe that what is good for the company is always good for the family, and not necessarily vice versa. We act

accordingly and expect the same from all people that work with and for us, external stakeholders included.

5. We strive toward profitability in all meanings of the word, included meaningfulness, sharing, and a non-zero-sum interaction with our surroundings.

6. Our Next Generations will get maximal chances in life, education, and possibilities for personal growth in exchange for their commitment, hard work, and passion to do a good job, whatever that job is.

7. In-laws will not work in our company but will be supported to find their best possible path in their (work)life.

8. By being excellent, you buy your freedom. Freedom is defined by agreed-upon boundaries.

9. Profit is never the first priority but is the result of what we do.

10. We adhere to the quintuple P-model in the following order: People, Planet, Passion, Profit, and Pleasure.

11. Sustainability and innovation drive our business.

12. Our family@business philanthropy operates under the motto: do not feed them but teach them how to fish.

This charter will be revised every five years or upon the request of whomever in the family.

This Family Charter is agreed upon and signed by all family members.

We, the John and Annie family, pledge that we will do everything in our power to live, work, and grow according to the rules that are on and between the lines of our Family Charter.

2 Family Forum

Can you guess what the preferred topic of conversation is with business families? Tadaa...Tadaa. The family@business.

Now, this is normal and completely understandable. If the company is still young (Phase 1 and 2, see Chapter 2) and G1 spends an enormous amount of time and energy to help the company move forward, it is quite normal that most conversations are about the company. Office and kitchen are intertwined. Family matters are discussed at the office and business matters are discussed at the kitchen table.

In phases 3–4, and certainly in phase 5, it is better to have a different policy. In these phases, the advice is to create discussion platforms where business is discussed in the office and family is discussed at home. But let's be realistic. For a family@business it is almost impossible to completely separate family and business matters.

This is where the Family Forum comes in handy. A family forum is an organized structure that allows all stakeholders in the family to come together to get information about the company. The whole family will then be able to put forward their own ideas and concerns, especially with regard to the company's policies that affect the family's participation in the company.

The Family Forum is a platform where everything that has to do with the family, the business, and the family@business that does not belong either in the office or in the home of the family can be discussed. Most business families that have set up a family forum organize these meetings in a neutral place such as a hotel or resort. The content of what is discussed in the Family Forum depends on the topics that the family members raise. A Family Forum can be chaired by an elected family member, or by rotating presidents. Some families invite an external specialist to take over the chairmanship.

Experts are sometimes invited to explain certain topics, ranging from financial and fiscal instruments to pedagogical best practices.

The Family Forum, if used wisely, is an effective tool to prevent possible family conflicts in the future. It provides family members with a structure and the opportunity to assess the current performance of the company and its management and to ask questions before misinformation is released or misunderstandings arise.

If a family member is dissatisfied with something, the family forum is the place to discuss it. This prevents the family member from expressing his or her frustration or emotions in places where it is inappropriate to do so. For example, an unhappy family member, someone who does not work in the family@business, who spreads his or her frustration throughout the family, or worse, through well-chosen parts of the family, can cause a dangerous rift that is harmful to the business. Another family member who, for example, works in the family@business and spreads his or her frustration throughout the office creates a mistrust that will be harmful to the family and the business.

If necessary, the family charter can be consulted to promote constructive communication. And constructive communication can adapt the family charter to changing circumstances over time.

3 Family Stewardship

In Chapter 14, we discussed the importance of non-family stakeholder stewardship. Now the time has come to detail the importance of family stewardship.

In the first generation, the family is still small but from G2 and certainly from G3 onwards, the numbers of family members may increase rapidly. Not all the children, grandchildren, and all their respective spouses or partners will be actively involved with the family@business. However, unless they sell their shares, they are connected as owners, directly or indirectly through inheritance and marriage contracts. This ever-larger system needs cohesion and coherence, or the family@business might go astray.

In the first generation and often still in the second generation, the owners-founders provide this by their parenting skills. From G3 onwards, it is necessary that this coherence and cohesion are actively supervised and maintained by other stewards.

This can be done in several manners and the best way is to find the methods that fit the best with your family's characteristics and needs.

Pater Familias, Mater Familias

The terms "matriarch" or "patriarch" are maybe a little outdated nowadays but the terms in themselves reflect an important reality in family life. In a family, like in any group, there is or are always informal leaders. Ideally, the informal leadership coincides with formal leadership. For example, the CEO is the formal leader and will be more powerful if she is the informal leader at the same time. The same goes for leadership within a family and especially within an ever-expanding group of relatives. Without leadership within the family, the risk for rifts, competing cliques, feuds, and even legal action against each other might flare-up. And that is to be avoided because it is bad for business and therefore bad for the family.

The Beatles' song taught us that "money can't buy you love." The same goes for the leadership within the family. "Money can't buy you leadership." Worse still, it can't even be learned at school, no matter how expensive your MBA program. This "X" factor of leadership can only be honed through commitment and life experience. But without its natural basis, there is nothing to hone.

In Chapter 5, we described the ten indicators of leadership potential and these factors touch the very core of the personality of a family steward. Mind you, this role has little to do with age but more with maturity.

Family Stewardship Tools

There are several tools that will help the family steward create and maintain cohesion and coherence.

The first is the most important: a personality that is blessed with social and emotional intelligence. An open mentality, great interest in the other, and tact combined with a small ego, ensure that the Mater or Pater Familias will be acceptable to the majority. A determined and decisive handling of incidents that threaten harmony, combined with a generosity that puts family members first, allows her to be present at all times without having to come to the fore.

Second, no fear of conflicts. The ability to allow conflicts to happen instead of smothering them under a blanket of love creates space for mediation and promotes personal growth.

Third, find ways to create togetherness. Extended families may not be able to have a regular physical contact in family forums or gatherings. Maybe a yearly family retreat can be organized. During these retreats, there is room for hanging out together, getting to know each other better in an informal way but also for sharing news about the business. You can organize a closed family website and online discussion groups. Elder business families can set up a family office to help them with their wealth management and even create a family@business academy of their own.

Why Family Stewardship Is Important

Individuals go their own way in life. They make their own choices. They encounter different vicissitudes in their life and react differently so that their path in life differs from all others. In short: Individuals individuate. This diversity is what makes us unique humans.

In a family without a business, the children have much more freedom to go their own way in life. Individuals in a family that runs a business together need to find the balance between finding one's own way in life and dovetailing into the family@business collective.

You cannot enforce a person to live and work in harmony with others. You can only invite them to do so by creating circumstances that intrinsically motivate their loyalty to family and family@business. When their sense of loyalty comes from deep inside themselves, it gives the best and the most sustainable outcomes. When there is warmth and love in the family, everybody just wants to belong.

Thomas L. Friedman teaches us: "When someone assumes ownership, it is difficult to ask more of them than they ask of themselves."

The family steward is the role model for this delicate balancing act between the good for oneself and the good for the whole. He shows the way and gives everybody the feeling of being seen and heard.

In this way, he creates a "loyalty machine" that makes it possible for everyone to feel at home in the environment of the family@business without having to put their personal needs aside.

The Patek Philippe watch company, a Family Business owned since 1932 by the Stern family, uses the following well-known tagline: "You actually never own a Patek Philippe. You just take care of it for the next generation."

The same goes for a long-lived family@business: "You actually never own a family@business. You just take care of it for the next generation."

This book has, until now dealt primarily with the family side of the family@business. Now we will concentrate on the business side of the family@business.

Chapter 17

Three Family@business Management Tools

Having studied the dance of the shareholders, both internal and external in Chapter 14 brings us closer to more businesslike interventions that are helpful in the succession process.

T.E.A.M-Work

From this moment in the process, it works best to fully involve your management team. That way you invite them to take ownership of the upcoming changes. Not all family@businesses feel the need to involve external consultants. It is entirely up to you to decide what works best for your case. John and Annie choose to involve the family@business consultants because they are convinced that their involvement has added value to the process. By the way, that is how it always should be: the investment in external consultants must be such that the costs pay themselves back over time. Remember: not all things that you can count are worth their while most things you cannot count are.

Dramatis Personae, the Management Team Plus Family Plus Family@business Consultants Cynthia and Mark

CFO: Muriel
  Head Marketing: Alice
  HR and Legal: Lillian
  Country managers: Bruce, Gunther, Alessia, Jacques, and Chen
  General Manager: Jerry
  Investment manager: Mony
  Business Unit managers: Monika, Andrea, Patrick, and Rebecca
  Family: John, Annie, Eric, and Cherly
  Consultants: Mark and Cynthia

DOI: 10.4324/9781003194200-17

Three Tools

The following three management tools fit precisely with the needs of the family@business in this stage:

1   Resource audit
2   Collective ambition
3   Business strategy

Once you've studied them, you'll notice how inextricably they're linked.

I Resource Audit

You remember Insoo Kim Berg's advice to always approach the client through his or her resources first? The organizational application of this solution-focused stance is that change works best on a foundation of what already works well.

When one combines this working hypothesis with solution-focused insights like the four basic rules ("if something works good or good enough, keep doing it or do more of it," see Chapter 2) and the goal orientation (Chapter 8), you create a powerful management tool that facilitates both continuity and change.

Corporate workers are familiar with the concept of an audit: financial audit, safety audit, quality audit, forensic audit, etc. The concept of an audit is not alien to them. Therefore, we introduce the innovative concept of a resource audit. Let's see how this goes.

John: *Dear colleagues, Dear Family, I am happy that today we can have this important meeting. Allow me to introduce to you the family@ business consultants Cynthia and Mark that have been helping us with the first stages of the succession process. After this, please introduce yourselves. Please add two things you did in your work recently that really pleased you.*

Annie: *John, why don't you start?*

John: *Yeah. Let me think. Last week I succeeded in not coming to the office during a full working day and not feeling guilty about it. I even managed to refrain from making phone calls and getting myself briefed all day long by you.*

Mony: *And when you showed up the day after, everybody was asking you if you were ill. (All laughing)*

John: *No, seriously, I have realized in the last months that I need to create more space for all of you.*

Muriel: *I do hope that you take your time for that because we still need your experience and expertise.*

John: *Don't worry. It will be slow and gradual. I learned from Mark (points at Mark) that before you let go, you have to grasp something else.*

Annie: *The same goes for me. We will take our time to meticulously prepare our fading out and your fading in.*

John: *So, the first things Annie and myself want to grasp hold of is reaching out for our future goals for all of you, our children, and the company. This meeting and the exercises that Mark and Cynthia will offer us are tools to get there.*

John introduces both Family@business consultants. Cynthia and Mark introduce themselves and explain the work already undertaken in the John and Annie family.

Then the management team present themselves. Some of them tell very nice stories about what they think they did well in their work in the last weeks. The atmosphere gradually loosens and a positive vibe appears in the room.

Annie: *Mark, why don't you explain to all of us the exercise you have in mind to kick off our cooperation concerning the management succession.*

Mark: *Thank you, Annie. Ladies and Gentlemen. In the coming months, we have time and opportunity to get to know each other well. For starters, we will do an exercise that built upon John's previous question connected to you presenting yourselves. First, let us take a little step back. You are all familiar with the concept of an audit, aren't you?*

Mony (investment manager) and Muriel (CFO): *Sure, that is our core business. We find what is wrong, where the gap is, what the cause of this is – the Why – correct this so the gap is filled. Bingo, ready.*

Mark:	*Yes, that is how we all are trained to do this. Today we offer you an audit that is a little different.*
John:	*Colleagues, the mind is like a parachute: it only functions when open. It took some explication from Cynthia and Mark before I understood the rationale behind the extra question to go with your presentation, ten minutes ago.*
Mark:	*Correct. Thank you, John. Now, we would like you to do a special form of audit, a resource audit. Cynthia?*
Cynthia:	*Let me explain. We use the solution-focused approach when dealing with all kinds of organizational issues.*
Bruce (country manager):	*What's new in that? We all work all day long towards solutions.*
Cynthia:	*Sure. The solution-focused approach doesn't go against that, on the contrary. It's just a different approach route. An alternative terminology could be "solution building." The idea is that change works best on the foundation of what still goes well. In a resource audit, we ask you to think and answer the following questions: "in spite of everything that should be different as of yesterday...*
Bruce (country manager):	*(chuckling) I could give you a long list of those things within a minute...*
Cynthia:	*...what are the things that you do so well that you will certainly keep doing them? What are the things that your team does so well that you will support them to keep doing them? What are the things that your family@business as a consortium does so well, that you will support it in doing more of what works?*
Bruce:	*Do I understand it correctly that you want us to think about things we do that in spite of existing*

	problems, are helpful for ourselves, our team, and the company as a whole.
Cynthia:	*Correct.*
Bruce:	*Interesting. And a whole different approach than what we are used to do, e.g. hunting for problems, shortcoming, and the reasons behind those.*
Cynthia:	*That is called problem-solving. It looks to problems in the past and constructs solutions for them in the today. The resource audit points towards the future that can be built upon the discovered -or should I say: uncovered – resources of all parties involved. That is much more future-oriented.*
Mark:	*OK. This is what we want to invite you to do: take some time to think about the way you go about your work. Jot down your personal ideas about the following questions: 1/what is it that I do in my work that works so well, that I will keep doing it; 2/what is it that my team or department or business unit or country team is doing so well that they will keep doing it and 3/what is it that our family@business is doing so well that we need to keep this going? We will take fifteen minutes in private and after that I propose that we present our findings to each other and discuss them.*
Jerry:	*What do we get out of this?*
Mark:	*A clear view on the basis that you can use as platform to initiate the necessary changes.*
Cynthia:	*You will also get a clear view on what it is that you just need to keep doing because what you do works well or at least – for the time being – good enough.*
Mark:	*Next we will ask you: what is it that you want to accomplish in the coming period? You can use the same question for your team, business unit, or country and then, overarching, for the whole of your family@business. Again, we will take fifteen minutes and then discuss the three levels and see where you concur or differ.*
Cynthia:	*After that, we will help you connect the dots: what are the resources that we already have that we can use to obtain our goals.*

Jerry:	*Yes, and we will also see what we lack and what we need to do to fill that gap. This is a clever exercise, cleverly built-up.*
Chen (country manager):	*I am relieved that we are finally going to do something other than just look at shortcomings and then have endless discussions about the underlying causes. In a country where I have to build everything from scratch, I am better served by positive support. Count me in. Oh, by the way, and please forgive me if this sounds inappropriate: will the family join us in this exercise?*
Eric:	*Of course.*
Cherly:	*We are all in it together.*

The management team and the family take their time to do the resource audit on their own. Mark and Cynthia chair the discussion they have on the result of their individual resource audit. During mutual consultation between all parties and in all possible formations, the participants become more and more enthusiastic about this exercise.

Alice:	*Wow, the more you think in terms of resources, the more resources surface. It's energizing.*
Bruce:	*Now I start to get a better understanding of this solution-focused approach and why it should better be called "resource building."*
Lilian (HR and Legal):	*At first, I thought it would primarily and even only be useful for the human resources side of our work but I now realize its application is much broader. It also concerns other resources like our excellent recruiting processes, our market leadership in our software niche, our strong balance, just to name a few.*
Jerry:	*The long-term vision of our family owners plus their deep engagement towards all stakeholders certainly makes us stand out as a company.*
Rebecca (business unit manager):	*I am particularly happy that thinking in terms of resources does not stand in the way of looking problems and challenges right in the eye.*
Cynthia:	*That is an important remark, Rebecca, because it deals with one of the many misunderstandings around solution-focused work: thinking in a solution-focused manner does not mean that you have to become problem phobic. (laughter)*

Collecting long lists of resources as a goal in itself is rather pointless. Then you end up with lists of resources that no one feels ownership of. This is a waste of time and energy, or more bluntly: a waste of resources (sic). The goal of the resource audit is to introduce a solution-building mindset whereby the result, both in terms of content as well as the process to reach that understanding, is equally important. Resources are defined as: whatever you can use to obtain your goal.

The overall goal at this moment for the John and Annie company is clear to all participants: pave the way to the future with the next generation and keeping the business successful. The solution-building mindset that now is installed in all participants will become the foundation for the next steps when they work with their staff. To facilitate this, Mark offers the following proposition to the participants.

Cynthia:	*Mark and I are excited that all of you have been willing to participate so fully in this resource audit. Now you have experienced the power of the solution-focused approach. You have noticed that solution-focused thinking and working basically is common sense, albeit from a new perspective. No need for complicated theory, no need for convincing, no need for yet another brand-new management model. You all had that in your business training, ad nauseam. No, just doing what works.*
John:	*On behalf of the family, I would like to thank you for your full cooperation. This is a good start.*
Eric:	*I agree. Good start, but now what? What is the next step that you propose?*
Mark:	*We would like to invite you to perform a resource audit with your own staff, business unit or team. You can use exactly the same setup that we used today: what am I, my colleagues, my team/staff/division/business unit doing that works so well that we certainly want to keep doing? And then you can facilitate the discussion amongst them like Cynthia and myself did today. Since you know your local situation the best, this will probably prove to be even more powerful than the facilitation that Cynthia and myself did today.*
Gunther (country manager):	*OK. But I have a problem, Mark. My team is really big and I am simply too busy to do this exercise in person with my people. If I would do so, this would take approximately three weeks of my time, time that I feel I can't afford to be away from the daily business.*
Mark:	*Excellent! I am glad, Gunther, that you bring this up. As a matter of fact, for all of you that manage a big*

	team of let's say more than twenty-five persons, Gunther's remark makes me think of a working method that is even better than what we did today.
Gunther:	*(amazed) I don't follow you, please explain.*
Mark:	*Well, imagine that you do the resource audit with the core of your team members, let's say between five and ten persons. You explain the method, do the work, facilitate the discussions and offer them a chance to experientially learn from it. When that is done and they give you the same feedback that you have given us today, you know they are ready for a next step. This next step is that you choose, you can also ask for volunteers, of course, some of your staff members and invite them to take the lead in a resource audit with their direct personnel. That way you take leadership and offer them leadership to help each of their employees take up self-leadership. Thanks, Gunther, you helped me to hone this method. On top of the results of the resource audit, both content and process-wise, you help your staff help their employees to help themselves.*
Gunther:	*Wow, sounds complicated but thanks anyway.*
Annie:	*Ladies and Gentlemen, I think the bar is open now. (Cheers from everyone)*

2 Collective Ambition

"If you want to build a ship, don't drum up the men to gather wood, divide the work, and give orders. Instead, teach them to yearn for the vast and endless sea." Antoine de Saint-Exupéry.

In Chapter 2 we already discussed the importance of involving the next generation in making the values and norms explicit. It is vital that there is a foundation of shared values within the family if you want to create a sustainable cooperation for the future. On top of the shared values within the family, it is paramount that there is a foundation of shared values within your staff. Especially in knowledge-intensive companies, these shared values must form the basis for a collective ambition. Without a collective ambition, and here we quote Prof. Dr. Weggeman, in the long run, the organization will become an island kingdom where bureaucracy is rampant and passion is hard to find: staff members with an extensive span of control might create their own fiefdom with its own rules and regulations. You do not want that!

In order to entice in everybody a yearning for the vast and endless future in the family@business, we developed a practical three-stage missile:

First you ask all participants to reflect on their personal values and on the values that they perceive to be important in the organization Obviously, not all people can nor must share the same values. On the contrary, if you don't want to become a sect, a certain level of diversity is useful. Where these value systems overlap, shared values arise.

Second you ask all participants to reflect on the "why" of the company. What is the "raison d'être" of our company? What would the world miss if we were not here?

Third you invite all participants to build a collective ambition: what is it that we want to achieve with working together? What goals give meaning and direction to our cooperation? The meaning of the word 'goals' in knowledge-intensive organizations that are populated by professionals is specific. It has less to do with numbers and things you can count for the well-known reason that things that can be counted, often don't really count in life. What we mean with goals goes beyond mere practicalities and can best be sketched in a David Maister quote: "Create meaning! Help your employees to find the excitement in their work. Quality and productivity will follow."

To go beyond the tyranny of the numbers, we quote Kate Raworth: "Meaningfulness tops the addiction to eternal growth."

Solution Builders International, Staff Meeting

Family and top management are back at headquarters, some weeks after their first workshop in which they learned how to do a resource audit. All of them have done this exercise with their staff and teams. The evening of their arrival, they share the results with each other. Everybody is in a good mood and they look forward to the next step. Next morning, Mark explains about the three-step missile and starts the next exercise.

Mark:	*"Would you be so kind as to think about step one and step two and jot down what your shared values are. Then we will have a discussion in the group to see what common ground comes forward. In the afternoon, we will take the first steps to building a collective ambition."*
Jacques (country manager):	*I hope you don't mind but isn't this all a bit fuzzy and wooly?*
Mark:	*Sure. That is always the case at the start of this exercise. Pretty soon you will notice that it becomes more and more clear. Maybe some examples could be helpful?*
Jacques:	*Yes, I'd like to see how this actually works.*
Mark:	*Like in many, if not all, incremental processes, the voyage is more important than the destination. So, I*

	will give you some examples of companies that have been through the process. Mind you, the final result has more to do with poetry than with an exact and factual manual.
Jacques:	We all are very curious no, aren't we? (all nod)
Mark:	OK, there we go. "We recognize that this is a unique time when our products will change the way people work and live. It's an adventure and we're in it together." Who?
Andrea (business unit manager):	Apple.
Mark:	Correct. Only Apple would use the word "adventure" and "together." Microsoft or IBM would never use those words. Even the product design of Apple reflects this: no manuals, to start an Imac, there is hidden button at back of the screen. Some clients, who first use an Imac, do not know this and call the repair shop ☺. You want the next example?
Jerry:	Sure. A quiz is always nice. What are the prizes we can win? (Laughter)
Mark:	Knowledge, ladies and gentlemen, knowledge. OK, a special one for the petrol heads amongst you. "The best or nothing." Who?
Andrea (business manager):	Mercedes Benz. I drive one so I know.
Mark:	"Sheer driving pleasure."
Eric:	BMW. I drive one. And let's not forget: BMW is a family@business.
Mark:	These slogans are maximally purified and yet it is immediately recognizable which company it is about. Think about the hidden layers of meaning in those slogans. You can get a sense of the DNA of each company, not only in the products but also in the way the organization is designed, how they treat their clients, how they manage their personnel, etcetera.
John:	One of my best friends is second generation of a large family@business. Their collective ambition, they actually call it their mission and vision, states: "First serve, then deserve." And everybody knows precisely what it means and what behavioral consequences it entails.
Jacques:	Sorry, John, and I hope you will not take this badly. But that sounds totally woozy.
John:	Mark, can you give me some time to explain this?
Mark:	Sure.
Annie:	Condense, John, condense.

John:	*Two years ago, my friend needed a new general manager for one of his main companies. After a long selection process, two candidates were left. Both had a big CV, a wonderful track record, both were Harvard Business school alumni. Well, during the last interview one of them was asked what the first intervention would be when he got the position. He said: "What I do not get, is this slogan under the picture of the founder of the company 'First serve, then deserve.' As a CEO, I am responsible for the bottom line and I think that serving customers first before you make money, brings nothing for the business and only digs holes in the bottom line." My friend told me that his wife, a major shareholder because the company comes from her side, said: "Thank you, we know enough. We will call you."*
Jacques:	*Oops, heavy stuff. Now I understand the power of small sentences.*
John:	*Great. So, let's move and dig out our own collective ambition out of our expertise and experience.*

Dear Reader, take some time to reflect on the John and Annie's Company. In your opinion, what are their most important shared values? What is the long version of their collective ambition? What could be their tagline?

Now, Dear Reader, think of your own company or of the companies that you serve. What are your values, your long-term goals, and your collective ambitions?

The Collective Ambition for Solution Builders International

Soft and hard, **T**ogether **E**ach **A**chieves **M**ore.

This collective ambition has its background in the business model of the John and Annie company where the software component strengthens the investment -hard- component, where the cooperation with the clients has more the characteristic of an alliance than a mere vendor-customer relationship. Hence the word "together." "More" stands for progress, growth, and development. "Hard" in results, "soft" in dealing with people.

It speaks for itself that the tagline that summarizes the collective ambition is the end result of a long effort. For an outsider, such a collective ambition tagline is more of a sound bite while for the insider, it contains all of the values, the goals, and the pattern that connects everything and everybody. As with most things relevant in (business) life: the journey is more important than the destination.

3 Business Strategy

One of the most versatile and powerful business strategy tools which are exceptionally well suited for a family@business is the Service-Profit Chain.

Solution Builders International, Staff

Mark: *Cynthia and I are impressed with the work you all did together with your respective teams. How you connected the collective ambition to your personal and your company goals. And how you used the outcome of your resource audits to fuel progress.*

Cynthia: *I fully agree. In order to close the loop, I would like to discuss the Service-Profit Chain model with you today. Then Mark will help you do a Service-Profit Chain audit to first see where you and your company are already first in class and where you can still make little steps forwards.*

Jerry: *You consultants are really driving us hard, aren't you? Luckily you do it in such a manner that it does not come on top of our daily work.*

Mark: *Of course not. If we would give you additional work that has nothing to do with your daily work, it would be a futile exercise because we would use your time and energy without you gaining something. You have better things to do. What we offer you is integral part of your daily work, albeit from more of a meta-perspective.*

Alice: *You offer us all kinds of fancy words and concepts but honestly spoken, I recognize a lot of how we did it in our company when we were still a fledgling start-up.*

John: *I agree.*

Mark: *I am happy with your statement, Alice, because it shows we are right on track. All of you will recognize the following: faced with a complex challenge, you scratch your head, need lots of meetings and discussions, apply a lot of trial and error, and then, POOF, it is ready. Afterwards, you think: was that so difficult? Why didn't we do it like this from the first moment?*

John: *Yeah, but that is how it goes when you develop something. When you have found the solution, it often becomes incomprehensible why it was so incomprehensible in the first place.*

Mark: That is why we sometimes call our coaching and consulting work, the CS-method.

Annie: Que?

Mark: The Common-Sense method. (all laugh). Cynthia, would you mind explaining the basic Service-Profit Chain ideas, please?

Cynthia: Let's look at the PowerPoint presentation. If you study the flowchart while I give my explanation, this business strategy tool will become clear. We didn't invent this tool. All credits go to Heskett, Jones, Loveman, Sasser, and Schlesinger who published this model in the Harvard Business Review in 2008.

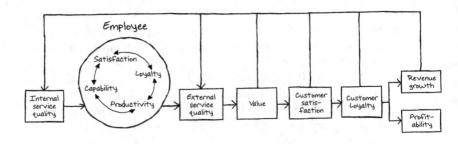

It's different in each company where the Service-Profit Chain starts. In first-generation companies, it often starts with the product, or more specifically the quality of the product that offers added value to the clients. Very often, the second link in the SPF-chain is the extraordinary care that is given to the clients, or more specifically to the satisfaction of the clients. This double care, product quality coupled to added value for satisfied customers, creates repeat business and customer loyalty. Business people, certainly when they operate in a knowledge intense environment, know that customer loyalty increases both profitability and revenue growth. Since most family@businesses go for the long haul and not for the fast buck, they tend to plough their profits back into the company. These investments they use to enhance the internal quality by creating state-of-the-art working places, high-quality support services, ditto product development, and policies that enable employees to deliver results to the customers. Even in times of personnel scarcity, these companies have little or no trouble in finding new employees. Investing in training and coaching lifts employee satisfaction and this turns them into even more loyal professionals with a higher productivity. And to close the loop, or rather to finalize the Möbius ring of the SPF-chain, this results in better products and services for the clients who ... and so forth.

John:	That is the long, more complicated, and probably more expensive (smiles at Cynthia) version of my friend's collective ambition: "First serve, then deserve."
Annie:	And it is an exact description of how we did it ourselves. John had this idea for the software program that would help construction companies streamline their operations.
John:	I remember our first customer, who by the way is still today in our top ten most profitable customers. When I first presented her the software, she told me it was too complicated and wouldn't work. I agreed with her that it was too complicated, it was part of my PhD. So, it had to at least look complicated. (smiles) I revamped the interface. After presenting the new interface, she told me she liked it but also that she was convinced that it wouldn't work. I was so sure it worked that I offered her to do one construction site for free. I have never told her how much time and work went into that first project.
Annie:	I remember that sharply. You were no fun for months in a row. Anyway, you did a great job and it has launched the company.
John:	Oh, yes, it sure did. The client raved about it and referred several of her non-competitors in the construction business to us. That led to projects in the petrochemical industry and from there on we expanded rapidly.
Lillian (HR and Legal):	From the start, we always invested in training and coaching for our employees. Some of them have been working for our company from the very beginning. Staff turnover and absenteeism has always been one of the lowest in the industry. Happy employees are loyal and more productive.
Jerry:	And that has an immediate effect on client satisfaction for the simple reason that we are constantly interacting with our clients. Some of our engineers even have office space at the client's facilities.
Rebecca (business unit manager):	Cynthia and Mark, can I ask you a question?
Cynthia:	Sure.
Rebecca:	When you look at our organogram, what function is lacking?
Cynthia:	Mm, let me think …
Mark:	Oh, I see. There is no sales management.
Rebecca:	Correct. We simply do not need sales managers. Like the name of our company says, we don't sell anything. We build solutions for and with our customers. We cooperate so closely with our customers that we sometimes know

more than themselves about the technical side of their operations.

Jerry: *Once a customer has experienced our level of product and service quality, they become loyal customers. Pricewise they know we are not the cheapest but they also know that we bring added value for a fair price.*

The Usefulness Question

Mark: *What Cynthia offered you in terms of the Service-Profit Chain model, is that useful to you?*

John: *Certainly. Your model describes what we have done on a more intuitive level.*

Mark: *What else?*

John: *When you distinguish all those different links in the chain, it becomes easier to study each link in-depth. That helps you kill two birds with one stone. You have an almost immediate overview of the status of your company as a whole, of each operational unit in it, of which link needs attention, and which link just needs to keep doing what is already doing well. Well, that is a lot of birds. (chuckles)*

Mark: *What else?*

Jerry: *Since it is a chain model it is good to keep in mind that the chain is only as strong as its weakest link. Detecting the weak or weaker links makes it possible to prepare for contingency plans. Then you know what to do if anything goes wrong.*

Mark: *In what John just said, you probably have recognized one of the three basic rules of the solution-focused approach. And in what Jerry mentioned, you have seen that the "why" or "who's fault" question, is replaced by the "how to" question.*

Cynthia: *This team sure is picking up on the solution-focused approach.*

The Service-Profit Chain Audit

Mark: *It pleases me that you all find so much recognition in this. From what I know of your company, Solution Builders International, it occurs to me that you are already using most of the components of this versatile SPC model. There is a great way for further honing the effectivity and efficiency of your company. We call it the Service-Profit Chain Audit. Connect the data from your resources audit to your goals and match these against your in-depth study of the quality of each link in the chain. Then identify what goes well or good enough and identify where you would like to make additional progress. When doing this, check continuously that your findings are in line with your collective* ambition. *Since it is a chain model, it does not really matter where you start. Oh and, don't forget to take into account the connection between each of the links.*

Jerry: *This sounds very logical. Can you give us a practical example?*

Mark: *Sure. One of your major resources as a team is that you are very good in cooperation. When making your business forecasts for the next year, you not only do this within each team, business unit, or country. You also create global forecasts, both on turnover and on cost budgets, that allow you to continuously focus your actions as you tune in to the many vicissitudes that are coming your way. When e.g. business Unit A runs behind the turnover forecast and this results in a loss, it doesn't need to be a big problem. Other business units can buffer. This can only be done when there is no internal competition. That is included in your collective ambition where you talk about team: Together Each Achieves more.*

Jerry: *I see more clearly now.*

Mark: *Another example is the Solution Builders International Academy that you have set up. You not only train newcomers, but you also offer some training to your customers. That is helpful towards client satisfaction and is promotes client loyalty.*

Jerry: *Indeed.*

We let time go by and see how the John and Annie family fare in the future.

Chapter 18

The John and Annie Family Business, Ten Years Later

John and Annie

Ten years later. John is 67 and Annie is 66. As usual, on a Saturday morning after breakfast, they sit across from each other at the table on their veranda and read the newspapers. It's their beloved moment to reminisce and let their conversation go its own way.

Annie: *Times flies.*

John: *Don't tell me. Care for some more tea, darling?*

Annie: *No thanks. I'm thinking it is already ten years that you gradually stepped down as CEO. That was a tough period.*

John: *I am glad it is over and that things at the company have settled in a nice balance. Well, that is, until they come up with the next new investment project.*

Annie: *You shouldn't worry, well, not too much anyhow. By now they have a track record of successes.*

John: *I agree but remember eight years ago, when I had to intervene.*

Annie: *I remember. That was a difficult period.*

John: *Looking back, it was my own fault. I put Eric on the CEO-chair too soon. And then he wanted to make a point by jumping into that investment project, although our investment manager was against it.*

Annie: *We were very worried about Cherly in those months. She was in a constant fight with Alice. When I confronted her with her unacceptable behavior, she quit her job on the spot.*

John: *Yes, and then she vanished. Well, she mailed us a note not to worry, that she needed time for herself. I don't remember what was the worst: my anger or my worry. Anyhow, when she showed up again after three months, she had the most astonishing news.*

Annie: *Indeed. It was both a shock and a relief.*

John: *Today, I am happy that she brought Pablo in our life. And in retrospect, we might have talked a lot more with Cherly about her personal life. We talked business too much.*

DOI: 10.4324/9781003194200-18

Annie: None of the kids are talkative about their emotional lives. But then again, they fare well. So why worry? We all have talked a lot about our eldest child, the company.

John: Annie, I never dared to ask you something.

Annie: Shoot.

John: Did you ever regret that we quit our regular, well paid and safe jobs and jump into the adventure of our own business? Did you ever regret that you did not sent me back to the office the day I came home, fulminating about my then boss who cut my project?

Annie: Oh, John, of course not. I cannot imagine our life without the business. It was hard work; lots of stress, calculated risks and it sure absorbed the most of our time and energy. But we got back so much from it. I can't imagine you in a career from nine-to-five for decades. Mind you, these people are absolutely important and necessary. They work for us. Without them, we never could have succeeded. But it just simply is not you, John, not you.

John: Annie, thank you. I could never have done it without you. I know I made mistakes and I deeply regret them.

Annie: Water under the bridge.

John: Maybe my biggest mistake taught us the most. Eight years ago, with all that fuss about Cherly, I was tired of it. In those days we still worked with our consultant Mark who told me it was too soon and to sudden to step down. I was tired of it all and did not listen to him.

Annie: (smiling) You didn't listen to me either.

John: I thought: Eric is 34. It now is his turn. And I announced this decision abruptly at a board meeting. You were there.

Annie: Yes. And I was as flabbergasted as the rest of the board. Eric was astounded. Jerry got up and left the meeting, slamming the door.

John: Luckily you intervened and ran after him or he might have quit on the spot. Wow, that was a difficult talk I had with Jerry afterwards. (Laughs). Jerry asked me what he should do if he was to be confronted with decisions from Eric that he disagreed on. I told him not to worry and he told me he did worry. I stood by my decision.

Annie: Didn't we go on a long trip just afterwards?

John: Yeah, I needed distance. So, we just packed up and left. Now that was fun. The first time I remember being away from the company without feeling guilty.

Annie: That was the time that I felt guilty about leaving. But you really spoiled me on that trip. Actually, it was very romantic. We were away for almost two months.

John: And when we came back, Eric told us about his investment decision.

Annie: I remember you coming home after your first visit to the office. You were silent, needed a stiff drink and shared your worries about Eric's project.

John: *By my sudden decision, I put Eric on the spot. So, I couldn't just come home and take my place in again. That would have been devastating for Eric's reputation and probably for our relationship. So, I let it go. And it almost shipwrecked the company. After some months of watching the unfolding of what I was convinced, would prove to be a disaster, I called Eric and we went for a long walk round the lake. I knew I had to be very diplomatic. On the one side, I realized that my decision just was too abrupt. I should have prepared Eric more for his role as CEO. On the other side, I was well aware of the financials that were looking bleak. Plus, Eric might not be aware that his project had more to do with proving himself vis-à-vis the staff than with a sound investment project. What have you? He was only 34 at that time. I apologized to him for the fact that we didn't discuss my sudden decision to step down and put him on the hot spot. I apologized for the fact that I confronted him with a fait accompli. I was careful not to criticize Eric or his project in any way.*

Annie: *Eric is not stupid. He obviously knew that something was up when you invited him for a walk. You never go for a walk, never have and never will.*

John: *Of course, he knew something was up. After my apologies, he asked me: "Dad, why don't you just say what you want to say." I kept walking and was silent for a while, maybe two or three minutes. Those were the longest minutes of my life. Then I told Eric: "once a decision is made and acted upon, the fact that the decision is made no longer is a problem. It becomes a limitation for which no solution is thinkable. The way to deal with the consequences of the limitation, no, that is a problem for which solutions are thinkable." Eric answered: "It is as if I hear Mark talking."*

Annie: *Indeed, I had the same idea.*

John: *Sure. Because Mark was correct in this. I told Eric that dealing with the consequences of a limitation is a problem. And, that a problem always contains a wish for change that can be translated into a challenge. So, I asked Eric: "if you think about it in this way, what is your challenge?" he thanked me and told me that he would need some thinking time. I wished him success.*

Eric

After his conversation with his Dad, Eric was both shaken and relieved. Shaken because deep down, he had always known that his single-handed decision on the investment project had more to do with positioning himself as a person and manager than with a sound business decision. Relieved that his father's respectful approach offered him a way out without losing face.

In the evening, Eric had a long conversation with Lars, his husband. Lars let him talk without interfering. After listening to him, he advised his husband to take his time.

Lars: *Let it simmer, Eric, don't jump to conclusions. Look at it from a broader perspective. What is it that you would like to see that has happened when five years from now, you look back at this period?*

Eric: *You are so clever, Lars. This is really helpful. I was concentrating too much on how to get rid this bad investment project. But you are right, I will give it some time and look more broadly. Plus, I will consult with some of my friends in the family@business club. Surely, some of them have experienced something similar. Who was it again that said: "If you are in a hurry, go slow." Although it is not as if the company is on the verge of going broke, I have to act fast.*

Eric spent a lot of time visiting and discussing with his network of business colleagues. Soon Eric was referred to an international equity firm that was interested in the problematic investment project. The family decided to sell the project. Although they had to accept a high loss, the sale freed them from that millstone.

Eric was concerned that his sisters would blame him for that substantial loss. *He talked to both of them and they both said: "You win one, you lose one. So? You solved it and we all learn from it. It will be beneficial for our future."*

John and Annie

John: *When I recount this period, I am still proud of Eric's accomplishments and what he did as a consequence of our little conversation.*

Annie: *Yes, me too. Although at that time, those two crises, Cherly and that project, were terrible. It is as if we needed those crises to happen in order to make real big steps forward. That was the beginning of a major change, both in the management of the company and in our family relations.*

John: *Both changes definitely were for the better.*

The Family@business Life Cycle, Phase 4

In Chapter 3 we discussed this phase extensively and you might want to reread those paragraphs. In that period, eight years ago, just before John took his rash decision to step down, he had been working together with Eric and the rest of the staff for some time. This is maybe one of the most difficult and delicate moments in the transference process. So many emotional, personal, strategic, and business issues need to be dealt with at the same time. Plus, since this is the first time in the history of the family, the persons involved and the company, nobody can fall back on earlier experiences. If you walked a mile in John's shoes in those days, you could easily understand the strain he was under. The same goes for Eric. After his Dad suddenly disappeared from the business battle scene, he had to fall back on himself. He was 34 at that time and his insecurity probably pushed him to that unfortunate project.

So, John had to step back in, which he did in the most elegant manner possible during a walk around the lake. John again became CEO but announced that Eric would be his Co-CEO. This allowed John some more free time and he could concentrate on the inheritance – and management succession process. Eric was much more open to John who took the time to coach his son.

The Family, Eight Years Ago

Cherly

After her three months of absence eight years ago when she was 26, Cherly, now 34, found peace in herself and her life. Her struggle calmed down when she met Pablo, an accomplished artist-painter with two teen children from his first marriage. They married last year. Alice was their witness at the wedding and is the godmother to their child Indra. Cherly took over the position of Alice as head of marketing.

Ella

She made her dream of becoming a urologist true. Now at 37, she is married to her boyfriend Max. They have twins of six years. Ella works in a university hospital.

Eric

Eric, now 42, became the only CEO after Jerry left the company a few years ago. Jerry left on friendly terms and became a consultant. Eric promoted two vice-presidents to help him do the work that he and Jerry used to do. He and Lars recently went through a rough patch in their marriage but with the help of a therapist, things start looking better again. Lars started studying architecture after he sold his successful import/export company.

Their daughter Esther (15) attends an international music school. The son, John Jr. (12) is at home but spends as much time as possible time with his grandparents.

The Family@business Life Cycle, Phase 5

As preparation to the transference process, the family and the staff did all the exercises we described in Chapters 11 and 14. Meanwhile, the family discussed their wishes concerning future ownership. For Eric and Cherly it was evident that they would become shareholders. For Ella, a medical doctor with a busy practice, it was different. Yet, Ella chose to become a shareholder too. After long technical, fiscal, and financial discussions with specialists, the ownership transition was done.

Eric proposed that all three would underwrite a shareholder agreement that would regulate how each of them could act. The parents kept 10% of the shares for themselves so that during their life, they could act as go-betweens in case of trouble.

Eric showed leadership by designing and installing governance structures. He proposed to create an advisory board where he and John would be the company's members. Together they appointed four external board members. Each needed to have a special background: international marketing, business development, merger, and acquisitions, and one needed to be an entrepreneur himself. This last member was a female entrepreneur that founded her own successful business and she became president of the advisory board. They agreed to meet each quarter and/or in times of crisis or opportunities. The members of the advisory board would eventually move to the Board of Directors.

Eric then proposed to install John as the president of the Board of Directors along with three external board members. This was Eric's manner of getting his Dad involved again, without overloading him with too much work.

Ella said she would like to take care of the governance of the family. She set up a family meeting every six months and combined that with a weekend away. For the third generation, there would be fun activities. For the second generation plus the parents, it would give opportunity for a family gathering with the add-on that half a day would be spent on discussing family issues related to their wealth management.

The Family Today

John and Annie

John (72) and Annie (71) are happy and content people. With a lot of time on their hands, they caught up with old friends, made lots of new friends on their cruises. They are constantly hosting weekends for the grandchildren. With every Christmas, the whole family comes to their country home. Every year Annie says that she wants new agendas for her and John so that they would be able to control their busy lives.

They enjoy the harmony and solidarity amongst their children and grandchildren.

Cherly

She and Pablo have a little girl, Indra, 7. Since the company keeps expanding, Eric invited Cherly to make the switch from marketing to HR. Her main commission is to supervise the recruitment of top executives. Cherly did a course in solution-focused coaching. Within the bosom of the International Solution Builders Academy, she created a coaching branch. She invited an international institute to provide internal continuous training in solution-focused coaching. Within a year, the company had access to a team of well-trained solution-focused coaches who, besides their normal job, could be called upon for consultations.

This coaching can be on technical matters but also on personal issues. The employees can choose with whom they would like to consult. It can even be done anonymously. Or, if people still find it too scary to work with someone from the company, there is a pool of external coaches that can be consulted.

Eric

He has grown in his CEO position, feels confident, and has turned into a real team player. He clearly is the captain of his team. His style is "leading from behind." Whenever possible he gives credit for all positive evolutions to his staff and employees. When a crisis occurs, he is on the frontline. Behind his back, the elder staff members lovingly call him "Little John."

Lars has his own cross-disciplinary architecture and design practice. He rapidly became very successful, specialized in high-end private homes. His studio works with six staff members and a group of about 15 freelancers. He travels a lot.

Esther, 20, quit music school and is in her second year of university. She studies economics.

John Jr., 17, does well at school. He tells everybody that he wants to become an engineer like his Dad and Grandpa.

Ella

Together with her husband Max and some associates, Ella, 42, founded a private hospital. Their twins, Aurora and Annette are 11 by now.

Ella took the initiative to round up some befriended family@businesses to set up a multi-family office. In view of the 35th anniversary of Solution Builders International, she headed the project group to prepare the festivities.

Solution Builders International, the Company

While it once was the eldest child of the family that had to be taken care of, now the company has many caretakers that act as loyal stewards. The company thrives.

Little Note on Solution-Focused Mediation for the Family@business

How to proceed when family members, for whatever reason, live in conflict? You can only have a conflict if you have something in common. What have feuding family members who are workers/shareholders in a family@ business, in common? The family@business.

Step 1: Allow all parties to – preferably separately – vent their emotions without taking sides.

Step 2: Find what is common for the conflicting parties.

Step 3: Ask each party what their goal is for what they have in common.

Step 4: Ask what they need in order to be willing and able to deliver what is useful for what they have in common.

Step 5: Offer recognition for their willingness to cooperate for the good of the company by congratulating them on their wisdom, openness, and goodwill.

If one or both parties choose conflict over cooperation, repeat sequences one to five.

What is the necessary precondition to succeed in this?

Put your Ego aside.

If no result, help them to face the consequences of their quarrel on the future of their family business, including their own emotional and financial loss. If they prefer a lasting conflict, pull back and advise them to consult their lawyers.

We realize that this section on solution-focused mediation is too sketchy and brief but an extensive discussion about this important topic would require another book.

DOI: 10.4324/9781003194200-19

Is the Solution-Focused Approach an Evidence-Based Model? YES!

In the world of medicine and psychotherapy, a lot of the interventions are paid for by public money and insurance companies. The method one uses needs to prove its efficacy before it is accepted as a quality instrument. The method needs to be evidence-based, in other words: you need proof that the method you use is effective.

Many clinical studies show that the solution-focused approach is evidence-based. In plain English: there is proof that it works.

A summary of research numbers shows us that:

- 168 effectiveness studies have been carried out.
- 50 Randomized Control Trials have shown to be effective, of which 28 prove to have been more effective than existing treatments.
- Out of 56 comparative studies, 45 show considerably higher effectiveness for the solution-focused approach.
- In 6000 cases, effectiveness studies show a success ratio of over 60% with an average of 3–6 sessions.
- Two meta-analytical review studies over a total of 43 researches show that, in comparison with the traditional approaches, the solution-focused approach delivers the best results regarding "personal behavior change."

Furthermore, research shows that the solution-focused approach is faster and lasts longer than the traditional approaches. Faster means that fewer sessions are required. Longer means that the positive effect is retained for a longer time and that there's significantly less regression. Something that has changed for the better after a solution-focused process will keep on changing for the better.

What is the relevance of these data for the solution-focused work with the family@business?

Given the importance of family@businesses and given the complex dynamics between the individuals involved, the stakeholders, the families, and the business in itself, it is of the utmost importance that the state of the art practices with proven efficacy are deployed.

DOI: 10.4324/9781003194200-20

Bibliography

Axelrod R.H. 2004, You don't have to do it alone: how to involve others to get things done. San Francisco: Berrett-Koehler.

Bateson, G. 1979, Mind and nature: a necessary unit. New York: E.P. Dutton.

Berg, I.K. & L. Cauffman, 2001, From couch to coach: lessons for therapists who want to move into the world of business. Workshop at Family Networker Conference, Washington.

Berg, I.K. & Dolan, Y. 2001, Tales of solutions: a collection of hope-inspiring stories. New York: W.W. Norton.

Carlock, R. & Ward, J. 2001. Strategic Planning for the Family Business. Palgrave.

Cauffman, L. & Berg, I.K. 2002, Solution talking creates solutions. Austria: Lernende Organisation, 5, 56–61.

Cauffman, L. 2001, Challenging the family business: the relational dimension. Oslo: Scandinavian Journal of Organisational Psychology, 2, 63.

Cauffman, L. 2003, Dancing the solutions shuffle. UK: Amed, 10, 4, 6–11.

Cauffman, L. & Berg, I.K. 2001, Belgium: Solutions Inc. D/2001/9314/1.

Cauffman, L. 2006. The solution tango: seven simple steps to solutions in management. Cyan Books.

Cauffman, L. 2014. 不懂带人,你就自己干到死:把身边的庸才变干将(新版) 畅销全球的管理经典！Xiron Books. (500.000 copies sold)

Cauffman, L. 2017. 不懂带人，你就自己干到死2：管理实务篇 《不懂带人，你就自己干到死》畅销全球四年后，作者全新力作！融合国际先进管理案例，内容全面超越前作。从低效到高能的员工改造术，36篇把庸才变干将的实用指南，手把手教你打造王牌精英团队 Xiron Books (150.000 copies sold)

Crichton, M. 2002, Prey. London: HarperCollins Publishers.

Csikszentmihalyi, M. 2004, Good business leadership, flow and the making of meaning. London: Penguin.

Davis, J.H., Schoorman, F.D. & Donaldson, L. 1997. Toward a stewardship theory of management. In: Academy of Management review, 22, 1:20–47.

De Shazer, S. 1984. Death of resistance. Family Process, 23, 11–21.

De Shazer, S. 1994. Words were originally magic. New York: W.W. Norton.

De Shazer, S. & Dolan, Y. 2007. More than miracles: the state of art of solution-focused brief therapy. Taylor & Francis Inc.

Forden, S. 2001. The house of Gucci, William Morrow Paperbacks.

Friedman, T. 2016. Thank you for being late, Picador.

Fritz, R. 1999. The path of least resistance for managers. San Francisco: Berrett-Koehler.

Furman, B. & Tapani, A. 1998. It's never too late to have a happy childhood. London: BT Press.

Gersick, K.; Davis, J.; McCollom Hampton, M.; Lansberg, I. 1997, Generation to generation: life cycles of the family business. HBS Press.

Goleman, D. 1995. Emotional intelligence: why it can matter more than IQ, Bantam Books.

Goleman, D. 2006. Social intelligence: beyond IQ, beyond emotional intelligence, Bantam Books

Heskett, J.; Jones, T.; Loveman, G.; Sasser, E.; Schlesinger, L. 2008. Putting the service-profit chain at work, HBR

Hoover, E. & Lombard Hoover, C. 1999. Getting along in family business. Routledge.

Jackson, P.Z. & McKergow, M. 2006, The solutions focus: making coaching and change simple. London: Nicholas Brealey.

Jaffe, D. 2010. Stewardship in your family enterprise. Pioneer Imprints.

Kaye, K. 2005. The dynamics of family business: building trust and resolving conflict. iUniverse.

Keeney, B.P. 1985, Aesthetics of change. New York: Guilford.

Keeney, B. & Erickson, B.A. Milton H. Erickson, M.D. An American healer. Crown House Publishing.

Kennedy, J. & Eberhart, R.C. 2001. Swarm intelligence. San Diego: Academic Press.

Minuchin, S. 1974. Families and family therapy. Cambridge, Massachusetts: Harvard University Press.

Maturana, H. & Varela, F. 1987. The tree of knowledge: the biological roots of human understanding. Boston: New Science Library.

McGowan, H. 2020. The adaptation advantage. Wiley.

McKergow, M. & Clarke, J. 2005, Positive approaches to change: applications of solutions focus and appreciative inquiry at work. Cheltenham UK: Solutions Books.

McKergow, M. 2021. The next generation of solution focused practice. Routledge.

Miller, D. & Le Breton-Miller, I. 2005, Managing for the long run: lessons in competitive advantage from great family businesses, Harvard Business Review Press.

Mischel, W. 2015. The marshmallow test: understanding self-control and how to master it. Corgi Books.

Nettle, D. 2005. Happiness: the science behind your smile. Oxford: University Press.

Olson, D. & Russell, C. 1989. Circumplex model: systemic assessment and treatment of families. Routledge.

Popper, K., 1972. Objective knowledge: an evolutionary approach. Oxford: Clarendon Press.

Shams, M. & Lane, D. 2018, Supporting the family business: a coaching practitioner's handbook. Routledge.

Seligman, M. 2003, Authentic happiness. London: Nicolas Brealey.

Simon, H. 1996, Hidden champions: lessons from 500 of the world's best unknown companies. Boston: Harvard Business School Press.

Tagiuri, R., Davis, J.A. 1982. Bivalent attributes of the family firm. Working Paper, Harvard Business School, Cambridge, Massachusetts. Reprinted 1996, Family Business Review IX (2) 199–208.

Walsh, F. 2015. Strengthening family resilience. Guilford Publications.

Walsh, F. 2003. Normal family processes. Guilford.

Ward, J. 2004. Perpetuating the family business: 50 lessons learned from long-lasting successful families in business, Palgrave Macmillan.

Weggeman, M. 2015. Managing professionals? Don't! how to step back to go forward. Warden Press.

Wright, R., 2001, Non-Zero: history, evolution & human cooperation. London: Abacus.

About the Author

Louis Cauffman has a double background. He is a psychologist, specialized in solution-focused systemic family therapy, and also holds a degree in business economy. He was the first to translate and use the solution-focused approach in management and coaching. For over 30 years, his passion has been offering services to family@businesses, big and small, domestic and international. He had been as a board member of the Family Firm Institute (USA) and still serves as an international senior teaching member of the Belgian Family Business Institute. Louis is the Founder-Owner of SOLT.E.A.M, an international training institute in solution-focused therapy, management, and coaching.

Louis teaches solution-focused management and conducts coaching workshops all over the world. He is proud to have been the first person to bring the solution-focused model to China, where he teaches on an annual basis.

The Chinese translation of his book *The Solution Tango* is a major bestseller in China, with over 500,000 copies sold. His second Chinese book, *Solution Focused Coaching*, is on the desk of 150,000 professionals who consult it daily.

Louis is Founding Member of the European Family Therapy Association, Founding Member of the Belgian Association of Trainers in Systemic Therapy, and Founding Member of the Belgian Association of Relational and Systemic Therapy.

In 1992, Louis received the yearly "Best Research Paper Award" of the Family Business Network, an international multidisciplinary association for Family Firms.

Also, in 1992, he was honored as a laureate of the "Académie Royale de Sciences, des Lettres et de Beaux-Arts de la Belgique" for his article "Challenges for the family business: the relational dimension." Louis has published eight books and 15 peer-reviewed articles and has contributed chapters to several books.

You are invited to explore our website at www.louiscauffman.com, where – using the integrated translator – you can enjoy all the content information.

Feel free to give Louis some direct feedback about this book; you can mail at louis.cauffman@louiscauffman.com. Thanks in advance.

Acknowledgments

Mathieu Weggeman
Jozef Lievens
Dennis Jaffe
David Lane

Index

A
accountability 45
adaptation 34
ambassadors 155
appreciation 66

B
Berg, Insoo Kim 12
birth 19
BLEEP exercise 55, 56
Board of Directors 164
business: community 3; ingenuity 45; organization 74; partner 34; strategy 29, 175, 185–8
business management 162
business organization 74
business-owning parents 31
business plan 68

C
change 158
change, adopt to 121
circular economy 149
client-centered approach 88
coach 79
cognitive bias 142
cognitive training 41
collective ambition 175, 181–5
combinatorial possibilities 129
comfort zone 121, 124
commitment 148
communication 52, 126
community 148–9
company: collective ambition of 44; re-organization in 93
competency assessment 50
complexity 19

compliments 98, 99
conception 19
conflicts 46
constructive communication 10
consultants 76, 101, 127–8
continuity 148
continuous learning 52
corporate investments 75
cradle-to-grave manufacturing 149
Cramer, Jim 140n1

D
DADD syndrome 130
Darwin, Charles 95
decision-making rights 10n1, 11n2
de Shazer, Steve 12
destructive communication 11n5
dynamic assessment 54–5

E
education: age-adequate manner 39; delay gratification 40; learning leadership skills 42; norms and values of family 42
effective communication 52, 125, 126
emotional intelligence (EQ) 45
emotional problems 25
engagement 148
entrepreneur 3, 68
entrepreneurial enthusiasm 25
entrepreneurial parents 26
environmental awareness 149
Erickson, Milton H. 75
essential skill 158–9
evidence-based model 84, 87n1
Executive Direction 164
external stakeholders 154–5

F
family business: accept conflicts 8;
average life expectancy of 4; biological
and emotional boundaries 73;
challenges 5–6; command 149;
community 148–9; compliments 9;
connection 149; constructive
communication 10; continuity 148;
criticism 9; defined 2; economic
principles 2; emotional aspect 160;
engagement toward 108; essential skill
158–9; financial and legal aspect 159;
Founders-Owners of 9; frictions,
annoyances, tensions, and
disappointments 8; fundamental
challenge in 18; gender in 22–4;
generation to generation 4; incidental
mistakes 8; informal rules of conduct
74; invest in contact 8; leadership 34;
learning process 8; life cycle of family
intertwines **21–2**, 21–7; long-term
consequence 143; loyalty and
involvement 4; management tools
(*see* management tools, for family
business); mistakes in life and business
7; overlapping systems 27; own values
9; parental authority 9; personal
convictions and values 9; personal
future 161; personalities 18;
prenuptials 142–3; psychological
aspect 160; relational aspect 160;
resilience 10; respect differences 8; role
confusion 27–9; stakeholders 34;
succession 6–7; tragedy 142; trust 7;
worldwide 3; worldwide statistics 4;
yearly appraisal interview **10**
family charter 165, 166–70
family constellation 62
family dynamics 37n3
family forum 165, 170–1
family goals 75
family hierarchy 74
family meeting 116
family members 34
family-owned companies 3
family stewardship 165, 171–2, 171–3
feedback 52, 157
flipchart 132
founder 37n3
Founder-Manager **26**

foundress 37n3
future ownership 195

G
gender, in family business **21–2**
Gerson R. 117n1
goal orientation 87
goal setting 94, 95, 109
goal-setting question 114–15
governance tools, for family business:
family charter 165, 166–70; family
forum 165, 170–1; family stewardship
165, 171–2, 171–3
growth 20

H
high-growth internet stocks 140n1
Homo Sapiens: brain development 1;
language and writing 1; symbolic
representations 1
human development 150
human interactions 7

I
impression 91, 93
incremental process 139
in-depth learning 17
informal rules of conduct 74
inheritance succession 6
Initial Public Offering (IPO) 136
interim non-family management 134–5
internal market 137
internal stakeholders 163
International Solution Builders
Academy 196
investment opportunity 50
investment project 192

K
knowledge-intensive organizations 182

L
leadership 34, 92, 138; continuous
learning 52; creativity 52;
determination and resilience 53;
emotional intelligence (EQ) 52–3;
feedback 52; learning 52; long-term
strategy 121; long-term vision 53;
optimism 54; pragmatic realism 53–4;

social intelligence 53; strategic
thinking 53; working relations 52
logical approach 103
loyalty 26–7

M
management buy-out 136
management succession 6, 35
management succession process 194
management team 150–4
management tools, for family business:
business strategy 175, 185–8; collective
ambition 175, 181–5; resource audit
175–81; service-profit chain audit
188–9
mandates 79–82
marketing department 104
maturity 33
maturity and intergenerational
partnership **33**
McGoldrick M. 117n1
mental marriage contract 22

N
Next Gen: adopt resilience and adapt to
change 121; comfort zone 121;
communication skills 121; learning
119–20; long-term strategy 121;
obsessive perfectionism 46; power
transfer to 36; preparations 123; real
job with real responsibilities 44; self-
awareness 120; self-confidence 120–1;
siblings 118; uncertainty 45
non-family employees 4, 27, 34
non-family family manager 136
non-family managers 32
non-family stakeholders 138

O
observable behavior 96
obsessive perfectionism 46
open communication 54, 131
overlapping systems 27
ownership: and exploitation 2; and the
financial security 159; and leadership
19, 36

P
parental authority 9

permanent non-family management 137
personal responsibility 144
Popper, Karl 54
positive thinking 86–7
possibilities 108
prenuptials 142–3
professionals 79
professional service provider 142

R
resilience 10, 112
resource audit 175–81
resource orientation 85–6, 98
resources 97

S
self-awareness 122
self-evident 91
self-monitoring 122
service-profit chain audit 188–9
shareholder agreement 164, 195
siblings 61–2
Simon, Hermann 3
skills: communication skills 23; soft
skills 51
social intelligence 53
solution builders international 30–1
solution-focused approach 72, 87n1,
101n1; consultants 76, 101, 127–8;
future orientation 14; goal orientation
14; in-depth learning 17; interview 89,
116; listening and talking 15–16;
mandate 14; minimax decision rules
15; perspective 11n4; possibilities 13;
protocol-driven models 16; questions
78–9; resource orientation 14; working
hypothesis of 13–14
stakeholders 34, 57, 139, 146;
ambassadors 155; external
stakeholders 154–5; and shareholders
147; stewardship 147–8
stewardship 147–8
stock market 136
strategic thinking 53
succession 146; family business 6–7; first-
generation entrepreneurs 65;
inheritance succession 6; management
succession 6, 35; practices for 68–72;
process of 158

sustainability 149
systemic thinking 116

T
The Henokiens 37n1
Three Circle Model 147
tragedy 142
traits 51
transference process 193
triangularization 77–8
trust: of employees 61; engagement and
    commitment 148

trustworthiness 26–7, 62

U
uncertainty 45, 157
un-covering resources 97

W
working relationship 52, 76–7
work in progress 50

Printed in the United States
by Baker & Taylor Publisher Services